What They A
Toward Happy+Fulfilled

"I wish I had read this book at age 20, age 30, age 40, and age 50. Professor Graziano does a masterful job of distilling the lessons of a lifetime and presenting them in a highly readable, practical, and fun format. You can spend 60 years learning the hard way how best to navigate through life, or you can read Professor Graziano's book."
- Robert Chess, Lecturer, Stanford Graduate School of Business

"Thank you, Professor G, your book came at the perfect time when I am dealing with a lot of topics that you address. Your personal stories so resonated with me. I feel like for anyone facing challenges, it provides a fresh perspective and a positive light. I'll be glad to have it handy for guidance as new situations come up. And for the time we're going through, it is especially relevant."
- Justin Ghandi, Former Student/Finance
Associate in Private Equity

"Dave does a great job simplifying some essential ideals to, as the title reads, live your best life. I have known Dave both on the youth baseball field and as an adjunct professor. He was great on the field and in front of the class, and from my perspective he has practiced what this book preaches. All of us could use some reminders along the way. Thanks, Dave, for giving us some shortcuts."
- Mark D. Schild, Assistant Dean,
Seton Hall's Stillman School of Business

"There is no longer an excuse for not moving towards happy and fulfilled. Professor Graz has solved this problem for you...read his book!"
- Bill Goss, Author/Life Coach

"Graziano is a business professor, but his commonsense life and career advice goes beyond how to get ahead. The pithy shortcuts in these pages will help you live happier, work smarter and find more meaning in your day-to-day, whether you're a recent grad or figuring out what to do in the next phase of your life."
                - Paula Derrow, Former Articles Director, SELF Magazine

"Professor Graz provides useful perspectives, guidance and personal anecdotes to ensure a healthy work/life balance. His advice helps resolve tensions between wants and needs, as well as ambitions and achievement, while including sharp focus on the passion necessary to balance it all. An engaging, yet thoughtful analysis of how to succeed in life."
                                                                - HGJ

"Graziano's book provides an adept guide to navigating the serial, lifelong crossroads decisions, with an emphasis on self-awareness. Why balance matters – and how to achieve this critical fulcrum – is the point of Graziano's classes with his business students. He has used those conversations and his own personal experiences as a springboard to sketch broad well-crafted lessons for any and all readers."
                                                                - JG

Toward happy + fulfilled

Professor Graz's
33 SHORTCUTS TO LIVING YOUR BEST LIFE

BY DAVID GRAZIANO

(a.k.a. "Professor Graz")

Zephyr Publishing

To my wife and daughter...

...the two joys and the two loves of my life, the "home team."

I am inspired by you both...you give my life a purpose.

Table of Contents

PART 3 – QUALITY OF LIFE

Introduction

There is an old expression, "Why is youth wasted on the young?" Maybe the more pertinent question should be, "Why is wisdom and experience wasted on the old?"

Throughout history, people have sought out a Fountain of Youth – since well before Ponce de Leon – in a futile attempt to reverse the aging cycle. In the absence of such a discovery, experience and the wisdom gained from living a life have always been the compensating factors that allow an aging person to remain vital in a youthful society. But wouldn't it be wonderful if a young person could tap into the secrets that are only revealed over the course of a lifetime?

Think about it: How many times have you said, "I wish I knew then what I know now?" Which is why I decided to write this book – to pass on what I've learned to my kid, to younger people and to anyone who has the desire to be reminded of some of life's wisdom before they're too tired to use it. Think of these pages as a way of cutting the line – a shortcut to wisdom.

The lessons contained here come from my own experiences as a stay-at-home dad, a business executive, a youth baseball coach, a community volunteer, an adjunct professor and a person. I've also included a generous dose of observations from others that have helped me along the way. I may not be an expert, but I've struggled in various ways that I suspect are very common in life.

I've also been unwilling to accept things as they are. While I've made my share of missteps, I try to remain curious and reflective, which helps me continue to grow. I've experimented and been a seeker, always looking to evolve. And I've come out the other side as a happier person with a life that feels meaningful and rich.

I didn't think of sharing these lessons until I began teaching business to college students. Interspersed within the course curricula of business strategy and managerial practices, I got into the habit of adding real-life perspectives on the course material along with bits of accumulated wisdom – hoping to prepare my students for the realities of both the working world and the adult life they were about to enter.

What I found was when I veered off-script into personal war stories, the students were more visibly engaged and asked more questions. Occasionally, I'd find these sorts of life lessons from the real-world would take up the entire period. And in end-of-semester feedback, I consistently heard that this element was the most popular aspect of the course. As a Business Strategy Professor tasked with teaching students how to find a "Competitive Advantage," I came to realize that these lessons were my own personal "CA."

To be clear, I don't consider myself wiser than the average person.

With all humility – and the recognition that it's smart to be aware of one's own limitations -- I am not promising to unlock any deep mysteries that history's superior minds might have overlooked. Rather, this book will focus on the issues involved in common day-to-day pursuits, such as getting a raise, or being persuasive, building a relationship or repairing a broken one. These are the types of dilemmas faced by everyone, whether 20 or 80, over the course of a lifetime. And it's important to have a reference point with which to approach such issues now – we only have one turn in this finite journey in life.

The thing is, wisdom and growth don't just naturally occur as a result of years passing. Many people not only stay in their lane but also stay in a rut, continuing to repeat the same patterns without learning from the experience. Have you heard the expression: "Do they have twenty years of experience, or one year of experience twenty times over?"

There's a big difference.

In fact all of us could use some help...despite the fact that a wise person once said, "No shortcut to wisdom. No tollways (or high-ways) to be wise." And while I agree that living through the experiences provides a deeper understanding of the lessons to be learned from living, I reject the notion that there is nothing to be gained from exposing yourself to a set of best practices for living, with the goal of avoiding some of the common life traps that derail us from living a happier, more fulfilling life.

At a minimum, these lessons can act as a set of tools to reflect or fall back on as various challenges and situations arise, and hope-fully there's something here for anyone to learn. Each and every one of these informal lessons has made a meaningful difference in my life. If even one or two resonate with you, I'll consider this book worth doing.

Part 1

Getting Started

1

- - - - - - - -

Adversity Is Actually
a Good Thing

I hate to be a bummer but let's get this one out of the way:

Adversity is a fact of life. We all have to deal with it. After all, if life was never bumpy there would be no reason for self-improvement, no need for faith, and no use for wisdom. In fact, if you never encounter bumps in the road, it likely means that you're not challenging yourself sufficiently or that you are not truly engaging with the world around you.

Nevertheless, this can be a tough lesson to swallow.

It also explains the need for this book.

Adversity comes in many shapes and sizes, including simple everyday things like a misunderstanding, a rejection, or a minor fender bender. Or it can involve more dramatic challenges, including losing a job, suffering a financial setback, getting a scary medical diagnosis, or dealing with the death of a loved one. If the global pandemic has taught us anything, it's that there's no telling what obstacles will crop up, and that none of us are immune.

Without these disappointments and obstacles, there would be no stories of perseverance or overcoming hurdles.

There would also never be growth.

Which is why adversity is actually a good thing, as perverse as it sounds.

Of course, sometimes it's easy to get overwhelmed at all the difficulties that come our way. That's when you need to keep in mind that unexpected difficulties are the nature of life and living. All we can do is to cope the best we can, reminding ourselves that tough times do not last, and try to be OK with that.

I'm sure you've heard this before. Indeed, there are countless expressions on the subject (some involving God, since spiritual people might reflect on God under dire circumstances). A few of my favorites:

- "Tough times don't last, tough people do"
- "God doesn't give you more than you can deal with."
- "When one door closes, a window opens."
- "People plan and God laughs."
- "Adversity does not build character, it reveals it."

None of these quips makes dealing with life's difficulties any easier or more fun. Inherent in obstacles and strife is disappointment – we feel let down in certain situations, with people, maybe with life, or with what the fates have dealt us. And when disappointment persists, it can lead to despair and chronic depression.

Case in point: At one point in my career, I was recruited by a friend and former classmate to lead a new business unit at a premier company. I had my concerns about the friend as being a very self-serving person, but I also was counting on the sterling reputation of the company as a good employer. I would honestly say I did some of my best work in this job – of building a team and getting this unit off the ground. However when an industry downturn caused layoffs, my friend undermined my position such that I became part of the layoff. Essentially my gut had told me not to trust the friend and hence the situation, but I logically talked myself into a challenging job that I wanted to do. And this was an experience that resulted in driving me toward depression and questioning myself.

This is a good example that there are actually two sides to disappointment, one being the hope that things would have turned out differently, and the other involving your expectations of the situation or the person. Maybe you did all the proper preparation for a task yet still did not succeed. Or maybe you expected a friend to be more loyal than he was (as I did).

In both cases, one part of the disappointment equation is the fact that you had expectations that were not met, thus producing disappointment. The good news is that the expectations are under your control – you can own that part, which can help you regain a sense of control and equilibrium.

Certainly in looking at my work situation, I couldn't have realistically expected my friend to do anything differently when the chips were down (in actuality I had more disappointment with the organization, as I had had higher hopes for their integrity).

That doesn't mean you can't have high expectations. But it makes sense to check your expectations to make sure they are realistic, or, at least, accurate. Is your expectation backed up by your experiential history with this person or in this situation? What does your intuition say about what to expect? Because if you check your assumptions, you can learn to tailor your expectations to the situation.

For instance, maybe you have a trusted friend who unexpectedly cancelled on a dinner date. Before you plunge into disappointment, reflect on whether there could have been a miscommunication. Or perhaps your friend has something difficult going on in her own life, or maybe they just have a history of being a flake, in which case it isn't about you at all.

It's important to recognize that trust plays a role in our disappointment, and sometimes (not always!) that trust is misplaced. Looking at a disappointment this way can help you regain some sense of control in your life, making room for a more hopeful outlook, instead of concluding that bad things just happen to you.

On the other hand, we all know that life brings about misfortunes – some devastating – that are not related to any "mistakes," misplaced trust, or poor choices. We can live a healthy lifestyle and still receive a difficult diagnosis. My mother had Parkinson's Disease and subsequently died of complications. And though Parkinson's strikes 60,000 people in this country each year, researchers still don't know what causes it. Life is hard. And it's not always fair (see Shortcut #2).

For better or worse, I dealt with the disappointment of my mother's illness and subsequent death as best as I could, mostly figuring it out along the way:

1) The only way I could reconcile myself to my mother's plight was to realize that some things just occur that we will never understand in this lifetime (though maybe we will in whatever might come afterward). In that sense, I took back control of this great mystery instead of letting it haunt me.
2) I attempted to mourn her passing, but who really knows what that means? Unfortunately, I got no help with this – I was 25 at the time, and following the funeral, my family generally avoided the subject of her passing. Instead of

letting myself truly mourn the loss, like many people, I tried to get back to my daily routine and make believe that I was unaffected, despite the fact that I was suffering emotionally in various ways. Because of that, my true mourning stretched out over a number of years as I resolved various issues. Looking back, I believe I could have taken a lesson from the Jewish tradition of sitting shiva, where loved ones stay at home and mourn for a week, while they are visited and tended to by others. This is followed by a formal year-long mourning period, where the living read the mourners' prayers and otherwise celebrate the life of the deceased. Thus they actively deal with an important process that can otherwise linger unaddressed for many years (if addressed at all), causing unnecessary emotional strain.

3) I made a conscious decision to reflect on positive memories of being with her before her affliction. Specifically, I dwelled on the good she had done with her time on earth, and all the unique traits that made her special. And I made a point of connecting with the positive traits that I had received from her.

4) I also learned a boatload from how my mother handled her ordeal – namely, with grace. I don't know that I could have held up the way she did but it was very inspirational. I thought about other good things I'd learned from the experience, including how my mother's illness had caused me to grow up more quickly and become super self-reliant. It also gave me a heightened sense of empathy, concern and a desire to help people who become disadvantaged in various ways due to circumstances (or illnesses) beyond their control.

Now let's look at "Life is Hard" in a different context, that is, *why* it is hard. Is there a reason we need to experience all the hardness of this life?

For such a profound question we turn to the noted philosophers Beavis and Butt-head, who were the main characters in a '90's-era cartoon series about two foul-mouthed teenage slackers, created by Mike Judge. Below is one of my favorites of their exchanges:

> BEAVIS: How come, like, some stuff sucks, but then, like, some stuff is pretty cool?
>
> BUTT-HEAD: Uhhh, well, if nothing sucked, and everything was cool all the time, then, like, how would you know it was cool?
>
> BEAVIS: I would know. You just said, everything would be cool.
>
> BUTT-HEAD: No, buttmunch. I mean like, let's say someone came up and just hit you upside the head? Well, that would be cool.
>
> BEAVIS: No it wouldn't. That would suck.
>
> BUTT-HEAD: Yeah. . . . [hits Beavis repeatedly]
>
> BEAVIS: Owww! Cut it out butthole!
>
> BUTT-HEAD: That was cool!
>
> BEAVIS: No it wasn't. That sucked!
>
> BUTT-HEAD: Yeah, but like, you know, after it's over, doesn't it, like, feel pretty cool?
>
> BEAVIS: Oh yeah.
>
> BUTT-HEAD: See, you need, like, stuff that sucks to have stuff that's cool.

Culture lesson aside, that is an insightful bit of wisdom. It's not quite the "meaning of life" but it does do a good job of explaining the condition of life.

The fact is that there will be stuff that really sucks, like my mother's illness. And there will be good things that happen – what we might call blessings – that we can only appreciate because those bad things happen. People don't learn much when they're winning. It's mainly in losing that we appreciate our good outcomes, and otherwise examine what we could be doing better.

Spiritual people might attribute the ups and downs in life to a grand design by some divine power. Atheists might say it's a matter of probabilities, that nobody has all bad luck or all good. To clean up an old country colloquialism, "The sun don't shine on the same dog's (butt) all the time," ...and probability-wise, it won't be all dark days for that dog, either.

The important thing is to embrace the dichotomy of blessings and adversity, and to face life accordingly.

I'm always amazed – and encouraged – by people who seem to consistently see the bright side of challenging situations. They view problems as opportunities, which they almost always are. People turn devastating events, like the loss of a loved one to cancer, into a reason to create a nonprofit to raise money for a cure. You *can* grow from a setback. Just as an athlete should do after a loss or a subpar performance, it makes sense to examine where you might be able to improve your approach. If it's a matter of disappointment, you might review your expectations to examine whether they were reasonable or whether they might need to be adjusted.

As always, take ownership over what you might reasonably expect to control – your expectations – and learn from that. And then

learn what you can from how things turned out. This won't necessarily spare you bad outcomes or disappointment, but you will
get better at handling them. And the resulting growth will surely
help you somewhere else on your journey.

> "If you would only recognize that life is hard, things
> would be so much easier for you."
> *- Louis D. Brandeis*

2

Fairness – A Matter of Degrees

We've all heard it a gazillion times... "Life is not always fair." *So tell me something I don't know,* you might be thinking. Yet this simple truism is at the root of much dissatisfaction, misunderstanding and suffering in the world. Maybe the saying should actually be: "What makes any of us think life is going to be fair?" Or perhaps, more profoundly, does it even *need* to be fair all the time?

I, for one, grew up thinking that life should, *of course,* be fair. Growing up in the '60s, I got messages from my father about how he had worked hard and seemingly excelled in everything, including progressing to reach a top position in business. To me, this sounded like a simple formula for success: Keep your nose clean and work hard toward excellence and you will get what you desire.

What he did not tell me is that there are bumps along the way, and that even he made some serious missteps, including with respect to corporate politics he had had to overcome. He never mentioned that there would be barriers not of our making, people who undermine us (intentionally or not), or that sometimes we're just the victim of plain bad luck or timing. The real question is: What do we do about it?

My answer to that is to avoid the trap of the expectation of fairness. If you are a "good" person who does all the right things and works hard...well, that doesn't always mean you will be rewarded with good outcomes. But if you were raised to believe otherwise (as I was), you will almost always be disappointed with the world at some point, or feel like a failure for not measuring up, bewildered about what to do next.

When I encountered a few bumps in the road in my career in terms of company politics, instead of rolling with it, I lost my bearings, questioned everything I was doing and experienced a true setback. I wondered whether the game was rigged against me, and it was impossible to win.

Instead of shrugging the situation off, getting back on that horse, and looking for another job where I could hopefully trust the organization and the boss – or otherwise concluding that I was not suited for large organizations (which turned out to be the more correct conclusion) – I became frozen in fear of another bad situation arising. I stopped looking for a new job, and opted out for a while. I felt like a failure, and I didn't know what to do next.

I spent the next year unemployed, licking my wounds and reluctant to expose myself to further disappointment by putting myself out there. And though I eventually got another job, I can't say I was all-in. Instead, I half-expected my new bosses would also turn out to be untrustworthy, that corporate priorities would shift on me again and that once again, I would be treated "unfairly."

I could have checked my expectations to see if they were realistic. Or I could have taken my experiences at face value and decided to embark on a more entrepreneurial path where I was in more control of my fate. Instead, I put myself in the position of being half-in and half-out, while failing to make a conscious evaluation of my situation – which was a poor approach on all counts.

I wish I'd known then what I know now!

It would be awfully nice if life was fair, but there will always be natural disasters (or a pandemic), mean bosses and petty co-workers. Not to mention barriers such as racism, ageism, and gender bias, all things we need to talk about and work on changing but that will always, to some extent, be inherent in the human condition.

Which leads me to another question: What's fair in life? Pretty much nothing. After all, none of us has had a hand in the circumstances with which we are born...our genetics, our family environment, the color of our skin, the socio-economics of our parents, where we live. And we deserve neither credit nor blame for any of these factors, which most certainly will play a large role in our opportunities. Is that fair? No. Life, for all of us, begins on an uneven playing field.

Of course, there are extraordinary people who succeed from backgrounds of poverty, drug addiction, incarceration, or abuse. These stories are inspiring. But the truth is, even though the playing field is uneven, we can help ourselves (or harm ourselves) by the choices we make and the persistence we exhibit. We still have a good measure of ability to determine how our lives go. Even if it isn't always fair.

> "Life isn't fair, it never was and never will be."
> - *John F. Kennedy*

3

- - - - - - - - -

Don't Worry

The subject of worry has been a common theme in culture due to its universality and its potentially debilitating effects. One definition of worry is the mind getting overly concerned with a situation or a problem, which is when you start obsessing about what *might* happen. Do this too often and it can interfere with your appetite, lifestyle, habits, relationships, sleep, and performance, leading to a vicious cycle of more worrying and more negative effects on the mind and body.

One approach to worry can be found in the Bible. (Note: while I espouse no religious views in this text, I have found there are many insightful and useful bits of wisdom in the Bible; I'm open to real wisdom derived from any source).

Matthew 6:34 says:

> "Therefore do not worry about tomorrow, for tomorrow will worry about itself. Today has enough trouble of its own."

This is very true since the problems we foresee for tomorrow often turn out to be nothing, or else they work themselves out on their own. It's also a call to keep the sources of your worry to a tangible and manageable level.

Of course, that still leaves us with worrying about today. My point here is to focus on the doing, not on the worrying. When you think about it, worry is a useless and non-productive activity – it produces nothing. And if you're doing your work, or your prep, or your studying properly, you should have nothing to worry about. I know this is easier said than done. The point is to keep worry in its proper context and not get carried away with it.

If that sounds too simplistic, don't forget how we defined worry: it's the mind getting *overly* concerned about a problem or situation. Ordinary concern, on the other hand, is essential to daily life and productivity. A life without concern is one of avoidance of anything that might challenge you, make you have to work, or make you uncomfortable.

So, concern is good. Getting *overly* concerned about a problem or situation, then beginning to obsess about the downsides to failure, well...not so much. Because when you stop and think about it, worry really assumes the failure part, otherwise what would you be worried about?

Some people do talk about a "productive level of anxiety," such as one might have before a performance, a job interview, a music recital, or a sporting match. Commonly referred to as "butterflies in the stomach," this sort of anxiety can help us focus on the necessary preparation so we can deliver to the best of our ability. I fully believe in the productive benefits of concern.

To take this further, think of concern as a mental checklist of things you might want to do to accomplish your goal, whether learning something, doing a job task, or connecting with someone.

For example, let's say you have a job interview coming up, you think you really want the job, and so you're concerned about it and nervous. What should you do? Everything you can think of to prepare. You'll want to learn about the company, what they do, and how you might be able to help them. If possible, try to learn something about the interviewer – what their angle or perspective might be, maybe even their interviewing style. You'll want to think of some questions to ask, both to show your interest as well as to make sure you have the information you need to make a well-informed decision.

Once you've satisfied yourself that you've prepared as well as you can for a job you think you want, what's left to worry about? Maybe you worry that the interviewer won't like you – but you can't control that, at least not at the pre-interview point (that's a worry for tomorrow). Should you worry about a trick question meant to throw you off? Again, you can't do anything about that except to maybe expect the unexpected and prepare for that, so that you don't get thrown off. If you've truly prepared by making yourself knowledgeable, and you know what you want to learn from the interview, then you've done your part. Most everything else is really out of your control. So don't worry about it.

Clearly, the distinction between concern and worry is somewhat subtle. And I'll admit that sometimes, not worrying is easier said than done. The point is to be aware of the potentially debilitating effects of chronic worry, then focus on taking care of what you need to do – studying, practicing, doing tasks, nurturing your relationships, based on your concerns. That's the productive emotion that leads to happiness.

> "Worry never robs tomorrow of its sorrow, it only
> saps today of its joy."
>
> *- Leo Buscaglia*

Two Rules: Show Up on Time, and Play Hard

When Joe Torre was hired to manage the New York Yankees in 1996 the news was not met with much enthusiasm among the team's fan base. He had had three previous managing jobs with no great success. The New York *Daily News* labeled him "Clueless Joe." Yet Torre proceeded to manage the club to four World Series titles in the next five years and became recognized as one of the great managers of all time.

While he had taken over what turned out to be a very talented team, he also had learned some lessons along his path (see Shortcut #11). One lesson was to simplify things for his players, boiling down his expectations of them to two rules:

1. Show up on time
2. Play hard

Nothing about curfews...or dress codes...or what to say to the media. Just show up on time and play hard. Seems like a pretty simple dictum and easy to abide by, right? But let's take a look at what they really mean.

Rule #1: We know what showing up on time means – arriving at your job/class/appointment at the prescribed time. But "showing up" also implies that you are alert and ready to go. That means doing whatever preparation is required to tackle the task to your fullest. That could involve studying, practicing, researching, getting proper rest, or something else, but "showing up" involves being prepared, fully present (i.e., mentally engaged and in the moment) and ready to go.

As for being on time, some consider that a relative concept. There are those who arrive before the prescribed time so they can allow for traffic, relax and be ready to go. Others feel on time if they're in the door at the prescribed hour, despite not being settled in and ready to go. Other people decide if they're within 10- or 15 minutes of the start time, they're in the game.

When Torre was talking about "on time," he was referring to the first group -- on time and ready to go. The second group, while marginally on time, are not fully present and ready to go. And the third are sending the message that their time is more important than that of their workmates/classmates/teammates as well as their boss/professor/coach. While it may not be their intention, they are being disruptive and disrespectful to the group.

You can make the argument that 10 or 15 minutes is not a big deal so why dwell on it, but I'm telling you – that's the message that is being conveyed. Further, that person who regularly shows up late has reduced their margin for error in performance with the boss or professor relative to the one who shows up on time.

Rule #2: Play hard sounds like a reasonable thing if you're a member of the Yankees. But what does the rule mean for the rest of us?

If you make a team, it means you have the skills to play the game, just like if you get a job, it implies you have the education, experience and ability to perform in your role. If you are accepted by a college, the Admissions people believe you are qualified to do the work. So, in these cases, too, just like any Yankee, you are bringing certain personal resources to the table. "Playing hard" means you apply those resources to the task with your full effort, staying fully present and bringing your best every day. Ideally, giving your full effort becomes a habit.

Showing up on time and playing hard makes a statement about who you are and how you go about your business, as you pursue something that is important to you. When you're doing that activity, you focus on the task and don't get distracted by social media and personal business. It embodies an attitude. In a career setting, these would be the first basics to professionalism.

Folk singer Woody Guthrie once said, "Any fool can make something complicated. It takes a genius to make something simple." Our two simple rules certainly contain a lot of genius.

By the way, it wasn't long before the nickname "Clueless Joe" was not only dismissed but became a joke about how much everyone had underestimated Joe Torre. With his two simple rules, he demonstrated his confidence in and expectation of his players' professionalism. And he set a tone for excellence that became legendary.

> "When you play, play hard; when you work, don't play at all."
>
> *- Teddy Roosevelt*

5

--- --- --- --- ---

You Can Stand Out by Doing the Basics

When competing in today's world, we tend to think it's important to have cutting-edge skills and elite training. As parents, many of us encourage our children to embrace learning and excel in the classroom in order to hopefully acquire pedigrees from elite schools. Snobbery aside, we know that more than anything, this sort of branding opens the door to more opportunities. We've seen over the course of our careers that a sort of sifting out process for coveted positions based on academic credentials is a simple fact of life in our times.

But once you get in the door, the question becomes: What do you do with the opportunity? Some people seem to think they've arrived simply because they've gotten a job (or been admitted to their college of choice).

The fact is, getting in the door is only the beginning. You need to produce, whether performing in the classroom, or contributing to a team effort or producing for a company.

It's easy to assume that "producing" means performing brilliantly; that brilliance is what is required to stand out in your new environment.

Think of Jonah Hill in the movie *Moneyball,* who shows his boss, Brad Pitt, a reimagined way for the team to compete through the use of analytics. He introduces the organization to a brilliant new strategy.

It's easy to believe that is how careers – or success – is made. But this is actually quite rare – and that is a good thing, since most of us don't possess those sorts of special talents.

I don't either, but I am good at the basics, as I will convey with a little story.

In my first job out of grad school, I was working as an assistant to a general manager in the company, an ascendent executive who could make good things happen for me if I did a good job for him.

I wanted to impress him.

I assumed that he'd challenge me to use the analytical and organizational skills I'd learned in business school to help improve the operation of the division. But what he really wanted turned out to be much less glamorous. Basically, every week, he would hand me a stack of memos from his Inbox (back when things were done on paper), and tell me to follow-up on every project and resolve any outstanding issues – i.e., take them to a conclusion.

Almost immediately, I found myself deeply buried in real issues that cropped up in the division, working with the company's operating managers to resolve them.

Once I got through a set of assignments, I'd be handed another stack of papers and a new set of challenges. Sometimes, I worried that the process didn't seem to tap my "special training" – my Competitive Advantage. At times, my tasks seemed fairly mundane, such as tracking down missing sales forms or getting a mistaken sales commission straightened out. But one of the first lessons I learned in my new career was that you can stand out in any environment by simply doing the basics. Or, looking at it from the flipside, most people fall down on the basics. This may well be truer today than it was 40 years ago.

At the time, I didn't think I was doing anything special. The only way I knew I was succeeding is that my boss would rave about me. He was amazed that I was getting so much done, and with very little help from him.

So, what "basics" was I doing? First, I was solving problems for my boss, making his life easier so he could focus on more important matters. This is a value-add for any boss.

Another basic: I was taking every assignment through to its conclusion. This is where most people fall down; they encounter an obstacle and punt, slipping the assignment to the bottom of the pile and moving on to the next. This is probably where I excelled most in my work for the GM – sticking with the assignment and, whether through persistence or creativity, completing the task.

A further basic: I treated people well and tried not to cause problems in the course of getting my assignments done. As my boss's emissary, I had license to push for certain things, but I was mindful of the fact that this could work against me if I abused it. So I tried to make life easy on people when I needed their cooperation. This is a basic lesson unto itself: If you're trying to get someone to help you, make it as easy as possible for them to do so. In my position for example, I might get things prepared before I needed to involve that person. Or if I was fixing a mistake someone had made, I didn't need to draw attention to the source of the error.

At the time, I was somewhat embarrassed when we would review my assignments and he would gush about all I was accomplishing. I thought I was only doing what he'd asked of me, and it was nothing anyone couldn't have done. But later on, when I became a boss, I learned to appreciate how valuable – and rare – it is to work with someone who does the basics well.

What are some of the other basics?

- Show up every day (see Shortcut #4), on time
- Be a good teammate and try to fit in
- Follow-up, follow-up, follow-up
- Do the little things that no one does anymore, like sending thank you notes
- Don't stand out in a negative way
- Look engaged (even if you're daydreaming)
- Communicate well so everyone is on the same page

Some of these values may seem passe, but I'd argue that's why they are even more valuable today. You will stand out simply by exhibiting these valued traits that are increasingly rare, in school, in the office, or anywhere.

The good news is, we can all stand out by merely doing the basics, and doing them really well. Any of us can do the basics, and this applies to any sort of environment. And it is a most encouraging concept to keep in mind as we tackle new situations.

> "Champions are brilliant at the basics."
> - John Wooden, Former NCAA Coach

6

Think

"Think" is IBM's motto. Corporate mottos tell outsiders, "This is who we are," reminding employees of the company's valued principles. It's my favorite corporate motto, which is why I'm adopting it as the motto for this book.

Most companies have apocryphal stories that circulate to reinforce a culture – whether the stories are true or not, they convey an ideal or a trait of the organization.

IBM's story goes like this: A new IBM employee is being introduced around the research labs on her first day. A week into her tenure, she says to a co-worker, "I can't help but notice Bill over there. Every time I go by his office, he's just sitting there with nothing on his desk, staring into space. What gives?" The co-worker replies, "Oh, Bill, he's a legend. One time he had an idea that launched a whole new line of IBM computers that was one of our most successful ever. They told him to keep sitting there and see if he could come up with another idea."

Is this true? It's hard to imagine. But it serves to illustrate IBM's priority on innovation and its willingness to invest in people and ideas, and to equate excellence with applying abilities to creative acts and solutions. And when you're in an innovation business such as IBM, that begins with ideas derived from original thoughts.

That's one meaning of "Think." My meaning is a bit broader - that is, to go through life in a mindful way, with brain fully engaged, learning and making decisions and choices thoughtfully. *Think* means bringing your brain to everything you do and absorbing everything you can. It means making choices in a thoughtful manner and being present with others. It means taking ownership in your role in relating to the rest of the world.

The fact is that much of the world does not operate or think in this manner. There is an expression (yes, another "expression", since so many contain universal truths and wisdom): "Some people make things happen, some people watch things happen, and some people say, 'What happened?'"

The majority of people fall into the last two camps. If you're not the person making things happen, it's important to at least be consciously watching things happen, as a choice. Because if you are consciously making a choice, that is a more empowering and happier place from which to operate.

So switch your brain on and leave it on. It won't run out of power. The more you use it, the more energized it will be. Try to learn everywhere you go. I constantly ask myself, "Why is this the way it is?" For example, as a person with an engineering mind, I constantly look at products and wonder why the engineers designed it the way they did. When I hear a bit of company news, I wonder what caused them to do this?

To my mind, there are three things that I want to do every single day: 1) learn something, 2) laugh, and 3) feel love. Life affords us these opportunities every day, so life is good. All three are important. But never forget to learn something.

Remember though, there is a difference between passively taking information in and interacting with it. If you actively absorb new information, you may learn something, or it may cause you to challenge the new info as being spin or maybe fake news altogether. And whatever you've learned, there is no telling how and when you might use it. And if not, you've still learned something...which is always stimulating for an active mind.

Making choices is another key element of thinking – of engaging the brain. People often fail to realize all the choices they have and instead abdicate decisions – either to a group, to "expectations" they believe others have, or to the way things have been done, to the dogma, or what's "normal."

To use yet another expression, "Why be normal?" Normal is comfortable but it's also kind of boring.

Instead, we can get in the habit of looking at a decision and consciously deciding: Does this work for me? I don't mean this in a selfish way but in the sense that there *is* a choice. The fact is there are many instances where the direction may not be our favored one, but where we choose to go along with the crowd because the decision is not a big deal and not worth the trouble. But again, the point is to do this consciously, knowing that there *is* a choice – a much more empowering place from which to operate.

Being present with people is yet another way to be engaged with the world. By *present*, I'm referring to bringing *your full self* to your interactions with others, rather than simply occupying the same airspace. We can pass someone on the street and look past them, or we can make eye contact and smile, and maybe make them feel a little better or safer (try it – you'll be amazed how positive this tiny effort can be for all involved). We can be on auto-pilot and engage in mindless chatter, or alternatively we can adopt a curious mindset where we're learning about someone, or sharing something about ourselves, and developing a deeper rapport or relationship. Being present will enhance all your relationships, while you learn things you'd never otherwise know.

Engaging your brain and being *thoughtful* as you go about your life is not only stimulating, but also mind-expanding. And the personal responsibility and self-determination that is inherent in this approach is a healthier place for the mind to live.

So, Think. Everywhere you go. Every single day.

> "The mind is everything. What you think, you become."
>
> - *Buddha*

7

- - - - - - - -

Question Everything

This next section is the natural follow-on to the motto "Think." It involves critical thinking or questioning what you are hearing.

Critical thinking was not so much a thing when I went through school in the '60's – we learned more by rote, which is not a very exciting (or useful) way of learning. However, if you were paying any attention to popular culture of the time (and you almost couldn't avoid it), one of the most popular slogans was "Question Authority" – many people wore buttons with that slogan. It was a counterculture slap at The Man, in essence, an attempt to chop the authorities down to size.

It's hard to imagine now, but prior to this period, people didn't question their institutions too much, whether the government, or corporations, or religions, etc.

Now, as we know, every authority is on notice, as we question not only government and powerful corporate interests, but also foreign influences, the news we read, social norms of equity and justice, social media, and censorship. This process of questioning is all healthy.

So how does this fit into critical thinking? One way to look at it is to say that the "Authority" we refer to represents everything as it is – the status quo – as well as the way it's being presented (a.k.a., the spin). So as much as I like that slogan, I prefer to say it more broadly: Question Everything.

What I mean by that is asking yourself things like, "Does this make sense?" or "Why is it this way?" Often, if you do some simple deduction in your mind or run some quick mental numbers, you realize that a statement or an argument is all wet. I don't know how many times I've gone through this mental exercise in meetings, only to realize that what I'm hearing is nonsense.

I remember, for instance, going through the questioning exercise when I took Organic Chemistry in college. Like many sciences, "Orgo" involved a lot of formulas that governed things, in this case reactions. Except in Orgo there were so many exceptions along the lines of "If you mix one of these with one of those, you get one of that...unless X, Y, or Z are present, in which case...." In terms of a science, I found this to be very troubling (maybe that's why I found Organic Chemistry so difficult to learn!). Ultimately, I concluded that it couldn't be real science because science tends to exhibit patterns that are fully consistent – without all the exceptions. And I further concluded that they'll probably have a breakthrough in the discipline of Orgo in our lifetime whereby they'll re-write the whole science.

The point here is not to highlight the sheer audacity and arrogance of my thoughts but rather the thought process itself. The fact is that the exceptions *are* inexplicable and do raise real questions, if you're inclined to ponder them (which I was, given my grade prospects in the course). By the way, Organic Chemistry has not changed in the ensuing 45 years and I have not read of any impending challenges to the accepted science. But you never know...I'm willing to be patient.

If I were to voice one complaint about the college students I taught (really, the only complaint), it would be that they didn't ask more questions or challenge me enough. I always encouraged them to do so from the first day, mentioning that I might sometimes go off half-cocked or get carried away. To my chagrin, it didn't happen often enough. Hopefully they were at least asking questions in their minds (like, "WHAT is this guy thinking?"). Maybe they worried that raising questions was bad for grade management. Regardless, I know it would have made for a more stimulating learning environment if someone had called me out on one of my theories (and no, I never told them about Organic Chemistry).

I hope critical thinking isn't becoming a lost art. It's healthy to question everything, to wonder why something is so and why it can't be otherwise. That's where innovation and progress spring from. And isn't it more fun to think, I'm in charge of the information I take in, and I'll decide if I want to believe this or not?

It's also necessary.

In recent years, we've witnessed "experts" make pronouncements about all sorts of things such as the economy, science, political polling, COVID-19, that turned out to be totally wrong. In some cases, they may have been operating beyond any true expertise; in others, they likely had a vested interest in taking the position they did.

That's why it also makes sense to ask: "Does this person have a reason to take this position or tell it this way?"

In fact, you might want to be skeptical when you hear someone hold themselves out as an "expert." I find that the smartest people tend to be the ones who underplay their knowledge, especially if they are leaders in their field. They are often the ones who are sufficiently humble and perceptive enough to understand the limits of their knowledge, and be open to seeking more. Per Plato's description of what he referred to as the Socratic paradox, "I know that I know nothing." That is, in contrast to so-called "experts," he does not pretend to know what he doesn't know.

As for information sources, press releases always have an angle, or a spin, to achieve some purpose. Your job is to figure what that is. Maybe it's to sell a product. Maybe it's to make the entity look good. Maybe it's to get out ahead of some bad news and position another angle in people's mind. But there is *always* an angle in a press release beyond simple information.

There is a lot of talk these days about the limited news perspectives many of us get access to – often a narrow band of sources that agree with your view. It's incumbent on all of us to seek out multiple sources and different views so we can come to our own conclusions. By the same token, if you read only this book to learn from an old guy what he gained from his observations, that would be a fairly limited perspective to draw from, too.

By all means, question this book. Question the information you consume (news, social media, word of mouth, teaching, coaching). Question the way things are done (how your field is conducted, the rules you "need" to operate under, the so-called norms.) Question authority (Why is this person in charge? Are they legitimate? Are the rules fair?).

One caveat: Please work an issue through in your mind before you decide to escalate it to the outside – you might decide you're OK with it or it's not worth pursuing (e.g., I never escalated my concerns regarding Orgo to my professor).

Other than that, questioning everything is a very productive, progressive, stimulating and empowering way of thinking. Don't be afraid to ask questions, if only in your mind. Think for yourself. You'll be amazed at what you might discover.

> "Learn from yesterday, live for today, hope for tomorrow. The important thing is not to stop questioning."
>
> *- Albert Einstein*

Part II
Interacting with the World

8

- - - - - - - - - - -

Selling Yourself

Before you skip this shortcut, thinking that the last thing you ever want to do is sales, please hear me out.

Unless you plan on living a life off the grid and have the means to do so, you will be doing some selling in all phases of your daily life. There is selling involved in making friends, applying to school or for a job, getting a loan, proposing marriage, trying to get someone to help you...every daily interaction, every idea you propose, involves a bit of selling. If you are part of the world, and you want to be able to be persuasive, these key lessons can help:

Sales Lesson #1: Focus on *Their* Needs

People think selling means talking, or having the gift of gab. Nothing could be further from the truth. Selling is about listening – focusing on the other person's needs – and then looking for a way to address those needs. This might involve finding some overlap with what you want – common ground – or tweaking your own idea or product to the other person's needs.

Think of it this way: No one buys stuff because it serves someone else's purpose. They buy something to serve their own purpose, maybe to solve a problem. So it follows, you won't be able to sell an idea if it doesn't serve the other person's needs in some way. Maybe it fits their view of the world, or it makes them look good, or furthers their cause, or plays to their sense of vanity, or educates them. We don't often think of it this way, but selling, when done right, is about *giving*, not about taking.

When you put it that way, selling actually sounds like a noble thing, right? And it can be, when you're coming from a place of helping others. If you accomplish something you're after along the way, that's a win-win. But the fact is that no kind of selling is effective over time if it doesn't focus on the needs of the other party.

Sales Lesson #2: Be Different

If you're trying to get someone's attention, you need to stand out from the crowd. That holds true whether you're trying to get a date or sell a product. Whatever your message, it needs to be distinctive in order to be heard above all the noise.

When I taught Business Policy (i.e., Strategy), I couldn't stress enough the importance of being different in terms of strategy. We talked a lot about Competitive Advantage, too. Being different in a way that potentially benefits prospective customers is something you can sell – and is a basis for Competitive Advantage. Or, if you're no different from the competitors, why buy from you?

That's one reason advertisements often use distinct voices in their ads, like announcers with British accents (pleasing to Americans), or fast-talking insistent patter, or even a jingle you can't get out of your head. These tactics help the ad get traction, since you're more likely to hear it above the rest – they get your attention. And if they're really effective, you can't forget them, even if they're annoying. That's what being different is about.

Not that I'm suggesting being annoying. But you want to develop a distinguishing feature, whether it's your warmth, the way you dress – something that will help people remember you. I stumbled upon this lesson early in my career, when I was hiring sales reps. I would interview a slew of candidates until one started to blend into the next. Beyond their technical qualifications, it was hard to keep everyone straight. The ones who stood out to me were those with some sort of distinguishing feature. It might be something innocuous like being extremely tall, or having a crazy-sounding name, or a pleasant accent.

It occurred to me then that my reps would have a similar challenge when calling on customers. That's when I consciously added "distinguishing feature" to my list of requirements in my hiring. It could be just about anything, but there had to be a reason I'd remember this person after they left the room.

You might find this silly, but I've developed my theories based on ideas sillier than this. And by the way, it seemed to work really well.

If you are applying for a job or for admission to a school at any level, just think about the person reading your application, who is likely sorting through literally thousands of applications and resumes. Most recruiters or admissions people actually begin with a rejection mindset, culling out the obviously unsuitable candidates to get down to a manageable number of possibilities.

So, the early rejects become the underqualified apps, as well as the ones that don't stand out in any way – the ones that sound like all the others. Your job is to stand out in some way, to be different, so that you can get a hearing. Maybe you might create your CV in a different format, or highlight an unusual experience, or lead with your best-selling feature. And remember, the idea isn't to perform some hokey stunt, but rather to do something that is authentic to you and which might stand out a bit. But by all means, be different.

Sales Lesson #3: Let Your Personality Shine Through

Revealing your personality is one form of differentiation. But this lesson goes beyond that goal.

What I've found is that often, people try to sublimate their personality to appear professional, or to avoid offending someone who might be turned off by someone with a strong personality. But in my experience, the people who are most effective are the ones who are most genuine, which means being open and giving about who they are. Remember, people buy from people they trust, and there is nothing that inspires trust more than genuinely being who you are.

It's also a lot more interesting to see someone being real than it is to see them playing some pseudo-professional role. There's no need to waste brainpower trying to guess what someone is expecting to hear, which often comes off as being manipulative (and gives selling a bad reputation). It's much easier and more effective to just be yourself and to focus your energy on the points being discussed.

In other words, just be yourself, and don't be afraid of your personality, or the chance that you might turn someone off. You could be more interesting than you give yourself credit for. And as they say, you can't be all things to all people. You can't hope to close every sale, but you can sell the people who fit with your interests, just by being yourself.

As a college prof who had to grade a lot of dry essays analyzing companies, I always perked up and paid attention when a student injected their own work experiences or thoughts as a consumer, shopping for the products sold by the company. I encouraged them to do this for their learning, and for my reading.

As a writer, I could have chosen to take some different tacks in terms of writing style for this book. I could have written in a more professional or scholarly style rather than with a familiar, first-person tone, or opted for longer, more complex sentences. And I could have written a longer book that elaborated on these various points and more points, as well.

But instead, I started out by thinking about my audience. I wanted to first sell potential readers on opening it, then on finishing it, and on getting some use out of it.

In other words, I thought in terms of *selling* it, beginning with Sales Lesson #1, focusing on my reader's needs. I wanted it to be easy and engaging, with a style that encourages people to read more, and that doesn't pontificate (like a Dad or a professor might do), or talk past the point. I wanted it to be digestible and relatable. Per Sales Lesson #2, I've attempted to include original thoughts as well as lessons readers might not have heard elsewhere, based on living a life full of both success and failure. And per Sales Lesson #3, I wanted to bring my own personality – my language, my sometimes off-kilter views (another point of difference) and a dash of creativity.

It is not my intention to turn anyone off to the selling process by breaking it down in a somewhat analytical manner. Nor do I want to destroy the idea of interpersonal relations by describing them in a transactional sense. Rather, I hope to make people aware that we are selling ideas constantly, and to do so successfully, it's crucial to think about the needs of others, to be different, and to always let your authentic personality shine through.

> "Everything you've ever wanted is on the other side of fear."
>
> *- George Addair*

9

- - - - - - - -

Don't Say Don't

Baseball Hall of Famer Warren Spahn used to tell a story about pitching for the Milwaukee Braves against the New York Yankees in the 1957 World Series. He was facing a tough jam with two runners on base, and slugger Elston Howard coming to bat. His manager came out to talk to him and said, "Whatever you do, don't give Howard a fastball up and inside, he kills fastballs up and in."

Armed with that "encouragement", Spahn went back to work. His first pitch to Howard was a fastball that trailed up and in. The result? A three-run homer. Spahn had a marvelous career but to his dying day, he would tell the story and wonder, "Why would someone give an instruction that was the opposite of what he wanted to happen?"

This is the best example of "Don't Say Don't" that I know of. It illustrates negative motivation, the power of mental imagery, and, of course, the resulting negative outcome to prove the theory that this kind of directive rarely works.

One reason: Who wants to be motivated or instructed with negativity?

Growing up, I mostly heard what not to do. *Don't make a mess. Don't take things apart.* (I would think that was the sign of a curious mind!). *Don't inhale your food. Don't stay out late.* When I finally got that boss who raved about my work, I only wanted him to give me more work so I could get another pat on the back. After years of negative admonitions, I naturally responded with enthusiasm to any positive feedback.

When I became a boss myself, I decided early on that I would manage the way I wanted to be managed. And later when I began coaching kids, it was clear that I would coach the way I would've wanted to be coached.

Anyone who has been involved in sports (or any sort of per-formance art) has heard about the value of positive imagery. A coach might tell their team to go to sleep and dream of scoring touchdowns, or of playing the perfect sonata at the recital. The purpose is to implant positive thoughts after acquiring the skills and techniques to be able to perform those feats. Skill + Imagery. It's a powerful – and successful – formula.

As a coach, I also listened, taught with messages that kids could actually use, and tried to make playing fun. And, more than any-thing, I made a point of keeping it positive. My goal was to offer nine compliments for every one correction. As you can imagine, I looked for any reason to offer praise, to "Catch them doing something right," as the saying goes. And when it came to the inevitable correction, I tried to always do it in a positive way (if you get creative you can *always* find a way to spin an admonition as a positive). I would also frame the critique as a necessary part of the team effort, such as, "We need you to backup first base on that play." The kids tended to respond pretty well to it, and it was a more fun way to coach.

Of course this lesson, like all of these lessons, are ideals, things to think about and hopefully strive for. Writing about them gives me a chance to review these ideals, and renew them for myself. As a human, I fail sometimes. I wish I could be positive all the time, and only spread positivity. But from time to time, I might find myself in a negative spin. So, I check myself, then try to get into a positive and constructive mindset. None of us should expect to be perfect; these lessons are meant to be reminders of what we might want to try to do on a regular basis.

It turns out there is a physiological reason why you Don't Say Don't, which is explained wonderfully in a TED Talk by Simon Sinek, as he expounds on how the smartest marketers connect on an emotional level. In his talk, he explains that the seat of our emotions – the limbic system – the oldest part of the brain in evolutionary terms, is actually what governs our decisions and behavior. It performs the executive function. And when we're faced with facts that might conflict with our choices, we might say, "But it just doesn't feel right" – because the new facts have done nothing to change the emotional state. They don't "move" you. We might use our rational brain to justify the choice, but our behavior emanates from the limbic brain. On the other hand, the more recently evolved neocortex is dedicated to processing the senses such as sight and hearing, as well as language.

So in the preceding example, the manager has created an image of a fastball, up and in. You now have the limbic brain that is using that fastball imagery to develop an emotion, and dictating behavior. You have another part of the brain processing language. The limbic brain cannot process language so it only sees the image of a "fastball up and in", while the instruction "don't" is sitting in the neocortex...resulting in Spahn's behavior being the high/inside fastball without the critical modifier "don't" getting involved in the process. It just doesn't work as it was intended.

So if you're trying to motivate or instruct someone (or yourself), avoid using the negative of what you're hoping to achieve. Don't say don't. Rather, you should talk about the outcome you're looking for, what it is you want someone *to do*.

When you use "Don't," it acts as an admonition – which is no fun for the coach or for those being coached. And in the case of Warren Spahn, he hadn't even done anything wrong yet, yet was told not to do it in the future – which feels way more limiting than being told what to do. The first approach forecloses options; the other approach opens up possibilities.

And couldn't the world use a lot more positivity, and fewer "don'ts"?

> "Don't say *Don't*."
>
> - *David Graziano*

Don't Live Someone Else's Life

Assuming you're paying attention, you might be asking why I would describe this Shortcut with a "don't" when I just said, "Don't Say Don't". You've just earned yourself extra credit.

One simple answer would be that it gives me an opportunity to slip in another point: "Rules are merely guidelines." They're not necessarily hard and fast, but rather guidelines that allow for a little leeway.

Another relevant expression you're probably familiar with is, "Better to ask forgiveness than permission" ...i.e., once you ask permission, you're stuck.

Having given myself permission to stretch my rules, the point expressed in this shortcut is more effectively conveyed with a "don't." If I instead said, "Live your own life," that would sound like an obvious, unremarkable and trite bit of advice. Who else's life should I live?

On the other hand, the phrase "Don't live someone else's life" is likelier to catch your attention and stir an emotional reaction (as in the Sales Shortcut); it conveys a negative image you'll want to run away from. If it catches your attention, you'll more likely ponder it.

We're all unique in our own way, subject to many influences beyond the home. You might say we're each a combination of nature and nurture in a random, jumbled-up sort of way. In fact, I always say that even siblings are raised by different parents – due to the effect of birth order, parents' cumulative experience in parenting, and maybe the parents being in different places in their lives from one child to the next. With four in my family (me being the youngest), I think my parents were more controlling with the first two of us and a little out of steam for the last two. Our family also had an improving standard of living as the years went by, making for another difference among the siblings. And with my mother experiencing a health crisis during my adolescent years and dying several years later, that also created a radically different experience for me.

All of these types of factors serve to shape who we are. And the point is that each of us is our own person, a unique individual with our own abilities, sensibilities, tastes, and interests. No one can fully take your distinctive personality into account, nor can they make good decisions for you.

And yet, so many of us try to live someone else's life. It can happen in subtle ways as the result of messages we've heard since we were toddlers.

It's not that our well-meaning parents were trying to give us bad advice or even to control our decisions (well, most parents, anyway). Parents talking about their lives in a positive way and telling us about how well their decisions worked for them is a very natural occurrence. They want to teach and be our heroes.

However, the fact is you are likely not the same person as either parent – nor any of your siblings, nor anyone else, however often you hear, "She's just like her mother!" Relative to your parents, you grew up in a different time in history, perhaps under different socioeconomic circumstances, or in a different location. And the world is full of a different set of opportunities now.

Which is why no one else is qualified to make your decisions – it's truly impossible for anyone to fully put themselves in your shoes, whether a parent, a trusted best friend or sage advisor. And why shouldn't you get to be the one making the decisions that affect your life? It *is* your life. (I'm not necessarily talking about when you are an adolescent and still fully dependent on your parents...although as you start to think about a career or life path, you should be allowed to have your own ideas.) But certainly, as an adult, all of us should begin to take control of our own lives.

That's not as easy as you might think, however. It may be you think you are taking control but there is history that you may not be fully conscious of, and it may be controlling you.

Take me, for instance. I was raised in a home with a father as a corporate exec, and I got the message that business was a noble thing, providing jobs for people, and hopefully making useful products. And I heard that corporate life was the biggest challenge and provided all sorts of opportunities. So, armed with an MBA, I charged out into the corporate world to work for a computer company. I wasn't terribly interested in computers but in 1980, I knew this was an unmistakable opportunity to get in early on an emerging growth industry.

Bad thinking on multiple fronts. First of all, when I studied computer architecture to help my new career, I found the process tedious – because I had no passion for it. And after some early years of success with good achievement and promotions, I ran into corporate politics for which I was ill-equipped (I still believed that life was going to be fair!). Plus, I discovered I had no interest in playing company politics.

After that, I tried several other corporate opportunities, thinking my first experience was unique to that company. It "only" took me 20 years to come to the conclusion I was not cut out for corporate life. I was too likely to challenge situations I felt needed improvement and had little patience for what I viewed as bureaucracy, not to mention the politics.

Looking back, it is clear to me I followed this path not as a well-thought-out fulfillment of my own interests but rather as a way to connect with my Dad, and to get the approval I felt I lacked and sorely needed. But regardless of what he thought, this was a fairly self-destructive mistake on my part, detrimental to my career, my happiness and fulfillment.

In fact, in grad school, I had taken a course in entrepreneurship (it was the first such course at Harvard; it was barely "a thing" yet). I really enjoyed the course and found the idea of founding and running your own business very attractive. But I lacked the conviction and the nerve to tell my father I didn't want to go the corporate route. So I let that passion fall by the wayside until later in my working life. Whether I belonged in business at all is yet another question – I've imagined several completely different paths that might have been very satisfying for me. We live and learn, and it's all part of our own personal journey. But that doesn't mean others need to fall into the same traps.

So don't do as I did but rather, learn from it. Parental or societal messages (or messages from friends, coaches or teachers) can be fairly insidious. And of course your parents, at least, presumably have your best interests at heart, so why not take note? Most children want to connect with a parent (or these other people) especially if they sense that connection and approval is lacking.

There are also subtle messages that society places on us – pressures to fit in and to act certain ways. There are pressures to adopt a common value system (and essentially reaffirm it). There is no shortage of influences that want to help you run your life.

In contrast, Bill Gates' story is a striking one in terms of venturing out on one's own path. In 1975, he was a student at Harvard when an electronics industry announcement came out about a revolutionary microcomputer being released. Having followed the developments in this area and knowing there was no software available for it, he essentially said, "It's happening. I've gotta go." He had hoped to be able to finish school, but he was also very attuned to this opportunity, with a clear vision of what he wanted to do, and with great conviction. So he put together a little software team and camped out near the client in Albuquerque to do the work that would put him on a path to creating Microsoft.

I find the first part of the story – where he was so tuned in to the opportunity – most notable and impressive. Maybe it's because when I was in college, I lacked such directed passion and conviction. Also striking was the support he received from his parents to leave school and seize the opportunity. They had always supported Bill's passion for computing and trusted his seriousness and ability.

Gates' experience has been emulated many times over by others hoping to grab the brass ring and fulfill their passions. Many have succeeded and plenty more have tried and fallen by the wayside, perhaps unaware they were not quite as talented, as visionary, or as driven as Gates. The key is to be aware of your passion but also realistic enough in your self-evaluation to decide if you can do what you hope to do. This is true whether you will be making sacrifices to do what you want to do – like leaving school or investing your savings into your startup – or just entering a new career.

While the points and the examples so far have centered on career decisions, this is only one facet of your life that should not be lived for someone else. This lesson applies to *all* phases of your life, including who you might date or ultimately want to make a life with (and probably even more so!). In the same sense that I was subconsciously influenced by my Dad's career guidance, I know that I experienced similar influences when it came to my dating life. I could have married the woman I did eight years earlier when we dated previously, if I had been free of an implied parent-provided eligibility checklist. (Fortunately, I got a chance to eventually get it right, though it took until I was 42.). More than any other area of life, your choice of a partner (or even if you were to decide you don't need a partner) must be your own choice, for your own reasons, because you're really going to live with it, every day.

The same goes for where you live, how you live, how you spend your money, who you associate with, and everything about your lifestyle. Live for yourself.

If you fall into the trap of "keeping up with the Joneses" – especially after this warning – that's on you.

No matter what path you ultimately take, make sure it's a path of your own choosing, for your own purpose and your own interests. No one can effectively choose for you, and you're the one who will be living with the outcome.

> "Your time is limited, so don't waste it living someone else's life. Don't be trapped by dogma -- which is living with the results of other people's thinking. Don't let the noise of other's opinions drown out your own inner voice. And most important, have

the courage to follow your heart and intuition. They somehow already know what you truly want to become. Everything else is secondary."

- Steve Jobs

11

Learn Everywhere You Go

I've already mentioned learning everywhere you go as part of the motto "Think." Learning is part of keeping an active mind, being curious, expanding yourself and staying stimulated.

I can't say if curiosity is an innate trait or if it is one that can be developed or practiced. I have always been particularly curious and don't know any other way to be. In idle time, I can look at anything and try to draw something from it, wondering, "Why is it this way?" I want to know something about everything, whatever the subject. And though I'm not a voracious reader, in spirit, I'd like to read every book out there that's meaningful. I'd like to know everything. I don't share this to portray it as any sort of ideal but rather to suggest there is a vast world of stimulating ideas and history out there that can make for a fascinating life – and for growth.

That growth might be reward enough for curiosity and learning. But there are also unforeseen benefits that will accrue from following your curiosity.

In his 2005 commencement speech for Stanford University, Steve Jobs told a wonderful story (among many) about a life lesson he referred to as "connecting the dots." He had enrolled at Reed College but dropped out after a single semester, feeling nothing he was learning was worth the financial sacrifice his parents were making. But he stayed around and dropped-in, or audited, some courses that interested him. One of those courses was in Calligraphy – a somewhat outdated art given our computer age, but a Reed Liberal Arts specialty. Jobs was mesmerized by the beauty and care involved with this ancient style of communication. Though he didn't foresee any practical application for him, he studied it out of curiosity and interest – because it was beautiful to him.

Ten years later, when Apple was designing the Mac, Jobs said, everything he learned in that course came back to him. His team designed the Mac to include everything he had learned in that course and the Mac became the first computer with beautiful typography (previous computers and printers had all used a primitive dot-matrix system to form letters). As he described it, if he had never dropped-in to that calligraphy course, the Mac would never have had multiple typefaces or proportionally-spaced type fonts. And since Windows only copied the Mac, it's likely these features would never have appeared on any computers.

Jobs concluded if he had never dropped out of Reed College, he would have never dropped-in on calligraphy. Yet at the time, he never could have imagined how this interest would lead to anything practical or productive. But while he couldn't have connected the dots in this chain – from his curiosity about calligraphy to the Mac fonts – as he looked forward, the connections were obvious when looking backward. Such connections occur, in a way that is sometimes magical and unforeseeable...and purely as a result of curiosity and passion.

I have seen this happen in small, everyday ways. Sometimes, out of curiosity, I'll read stories about companies' successes and learn about a new business model or capability. Subsequently, I might be advising a company in a different industry and be able to bring ideas from one situation to another. Of course, this also illustrates the point that "there is nothing new under the sun" – just a lot of recycling of ideas. But if I didn't keep adding tools to my bag, and let myself be led by curiosity to come across new ones, I would run out of ideas and not be a very good consultant.

Believe it or not, in 1899 the Commissioner of the US Patent Office, Charles Duell stated that "everything that can be invented has been invented." To put it mildly, he was a little off on that one. In the past 30 years or so, the level of innovation has only seemed to only accelerate, year by year. This makes it incumbent on all of us to be curious, just in order to keep up. Today's young people have grown up in this rapidly-evolving environment and assume things have always been this way. I can assure you of two facts:

1) things have not always been so fast-changing, and much of what we take for granted today did not exist when I was young, and...
2) as you grow older, if you do not stay curious, this evolution will pass you by like a freight train.

To give you a little perspective: The very first smartphones were introduced 20 years ago. We do all sorts of things on a smartphone today without thinking, but just 15 years ago, most of us did all these things in other ways – using maps, phone books, pay phones, encyclopedias, reading newspapers and writing and sending letters – we had none of this at our fingertips. Many uncurious people were late to the game in adopting the smartphone but virtually everyone has caught up by now as it has become essential.

So, as with the dinosaur, evolve or die.

On another note, we all have regular instances where, as we go about life with our ears and eyes open, we encounter some input that causes us to focus on something important to us. We look at it as a sign. Some spirit of the universe or some matter of fate has provided us with a message that we need to do something...call someone, try for a new job, forgive someone, ask someone for a date, buy something. Or perhaps it is something that causes you to make a leap in your thinking, a breakthrough on an issue that has been troubling you. We all have these experiences and they can be wondrous.

I don't believe these moments are actually due to anything spiritual or due to fate. The fact is, these messages are all around us all the time...it's only a matter of whether we are open, attentive and ready to see them.

You might literally bump into your soulmate on the street, but if you're not open to meeting someone new, that encounter is lost, like many other innocuous occurrences in life. Isn't that amazing to consider?

It seems like I coincidentally have the experience of running into someone I know in places I would never imagine, on a regular basis – I've come to pretty well expect it to happen. This seems somewhat unusual as I am not one of those people "who knows everyone". But I do think people in various circles tend to travel in similar orbits and that these coincidences are just a matter of being curious and paying attention. I tend to people-watch and actually look at faces. I think these "coincidences" are all around us, all the time...it's only a matter of whether we're paying attention. They are less coincidental than they are a matter of an opportunity met – or missed.

I have experienced "signs" that have helped me resolve issues that have been on my mind (for an example, see Shortcut #24, "Paris or Vienna?"). As I pondered how that message came to me at just the right time, I would realize that messages of that sort had probably been around me for years; I just wasn't ready to hear them. So, it's important to be curious, alert, and also open-minded.

In fact, this book is the product of just such a realization. I had been using all of these lessons in teaching my college business courses for years. I had also come to enjoy writing. And with COVID-induced cabin fever, I was looking for something productive to do with my time. But it wasn't until a conversation with a friend that the idea for this book came about. The pieces were in place to write this book and had been for some time. But it wasn't until I needed something to do with my time that I took a hint from an offhand conversation to actually start doing something.

Which is also to say that learning everywhere you go includes learning from *everyone* you can. I don't think there's a person alive I can't learn something from. My grandfather was largely an uneducated man, but one of the wisest people I've known, and I learned so much from how he lived his life. Learning from everyone you can means never pre-judging what someone might know or who they might know (e.g., when we're networking). When you meet someone with a different background than your own, it's a safe bet they have something to teach you. In fact, you might find yourself having a conversation that's more interesting and rewarding than you expected. Never pre-judge any opportunity to learn.

We all have messages, signs and learning opportunities all around us, all the time. We can recognize them or we can whiff on them. That is a choice. We can also choose to be curious, which is a prerequisite to learning everywhere you go. You may not be able to "connect the dots" in advance, but in hindsight, following your curiosity and your passions can lead to some amazing results.

> "Live as if you were to die tomorrow. Learn as if you
> were to live forever."
>
> *- Mahatma Ghandi*

12

-- -- -- -- -- -- -- -- -- -- --

Follow Your Passion

Passion might be the single most important factor in any success, whether in a persons' career, a relationship, a company or a cause. To my mind, passion is even more crucial than the quality of someone's idea, intelligence, finances, connections or any other asset. The reason? It is passion that pushes us to persist when we hit a wall that feels insurmountable, that helps us find a way to the other side of that wall – around it, over it, under it, or right through it.

Nothing great is achieved without passion – no great inventions, no social causes, no great organizations, no great progress, no great careers, nor any great loves. This passion begins with one person having a fervor for an idea, an ideal, or a cause...and if needed, demonstrating that passion will help them enlist others to make them part of the effort.

Interestingly, the word "passion" derives from the Latin *passus*, which refers to suffering. We normally think of passion in terms of intense enthusiasm or compelling desire toward a person or idea or cause. I think the real point is that passion makes you feel intensely, makes you feel alive, and experience both pleasure and pain in its pursuit. The joy and the suffering are two sides of the same coin.

There are countless stories of people who started out with faulty ideas, but who persisted and kept trying (and, likely, suffered) until they found a winning formula. Thomas Edison's teachers said he was "too stupid to learn anything." He was fired from his first two jobs for being "non-productive." As an inventor, Edison made 1,000 unsuccessful attempts at inventing the light bulb. When a reporter asked, "How did it feel to fail 1,000 times?" Edison replied, "I didn't fail 1,000 times. The light bulb was an invention with 1,000 steps."

In working on a novel storage battery, Edison ran 9,000 experiments without success. When a colleague commented about the lack of results, Edison replied, "Results! Why, man, I have gotten lots of results! I know several thousand things that won't work!" Fittingly Edison was also credited with the very apt quote, "Genius is one percent inspiration and ninety-nine percent perspiration."

Of course, most of us will not have the vision of a Thomas Edison or a Steve Jobs. But we can all be passionate about something and use that passion to team up with others who share the same passion.

It might be that your passion falls outside of your career. How many people do you know who mainly work hard at their job in order to support their passion of competing in triathlons, or traveling the world, or just supporting their families?

I believe the ideal would be to find passions to pursue in all phases of life...your career, your recreation, hobbies, your family and other personal relations. In all areas of life, it seems over time there is a natural tendency to increasingly place emphasis on the elements we are more passionate about, and then let the less important aspects fall by the wayside. With age, you realize time is limited so you make choices to spend your time pursuing your own priorities – this goes for activities as well as people in your life. The important thing is to seek out those passions for people and activities, and focus your energies on them.

I've always marveled at people who discover a passion as teen-agers and follow it into a field of study and a career – I think that is a real gift. But any of us can discover a passion at any point – I know that I've discovered a few along the way that have turned out to be very pleasant surprises, including coaching, teaching, writing and bobblehead dolls.

Mark Twain once said: "Do something you love and you'll never have to work a day in your life." (On a side note, it seems most quotes involving common sense or politics are attributed to either Mark Twain or Winston Churchill – whether the attribution is right or wrong, both were extremely wise.)

I like to think of Twain's quote a little differently: *Do something you love, or you'll never really be great at what you do.* The point is, in order to become really great at anything (and don't we all want to be really good at something?), you need to be somewhat consumed by it. It needs to be in your heart. You need to put a lot of work and focus into it (I explore this in the next shortcut). When you're passionate about something, you might find your persistence leading you to work out questions in your head at 4 AM while you're otherwise trying to sleep. You'll run into road-blocks that could make you want to give up. It is only with passion (and stubbornness) that you can sustain yourself through all of the challenges and maintain a reason to feel it is all worthwhile.

I *can* speak for working while passion is lacking. In my first 20 years of corporate life, spent mainly in the computer industry, I never wanted to think about work outside of my work day. I never wanted to study computing to add to my knowledge base – because I was never passionate about computers, per se. I did enough to produce good results in my work but it never felt like a life-or-death endeavor, and I never felt compelled to produce something over the top. Because I was a capable person, I could do a good enough job, but I never stretched myself to my full capability and I never felt entirely fulfilled.

When you are done with your own career, I don't think you will want to describe it as I've just done. Working without passion is no fun, and it will not bring out the best in you. I'll also note, however, that many people happily make that deal in the knowledge they are well paid, the time demands are manageable and it affords them the ability to indulge their passions elsewhere – either with family or other interests.

Some people, on the other hand, might find passion in a single aspect of their work rather than the industry as a whole or the cause they are working in. A salesperson, for instance, might just enjoy the thrill of the large ticket sale, regardless of the industry. A teacher might hate the paperwork and bureaucracy involved with teaching but fill up with joy when the light goes on for a student. But if you have a hard time finding *any* sort of passion and fulfillment in your pursuits, then it might be time to look elsewhere, as I eventually did when I moved away from corporate life into more self-directed pursuits like consulting, coaching and then teaching.

The good news is you get to choose and you get to figure out the formula that works for your life...tweaking it, reloading it, and trying again until you find something that does fulfill you.

> "If you can't figure out your purpose, figure out your passion. For your passion will lead you right into your purpose."
> - *Bishop T.D. Jakes*

13

Mastery in Ten Thousand Hours

The ten thousand hours concept is one of the most hopeful ideas for most of us with average ability. The idea is, with proper focus and diligence, any one of us can master an activity or subject. This doesn't mean we will become a world class talent – there needs to be some aptitude and maybe genetic predisposition for that – but it's possible to become masters of the art and know what the experts know. This mastery can apply to your chosen field, a sport, or a hobby. To my mind, this is a powerful concept for anyone with aspirations.

In his 2008 book *Outliers*, Malcolm Gladwell popularized the notion of mastery of a skill or subject by investing 10,000 hours of practice. This was not an altogether new concept but he brought popularity to it, and more importantly he defined and quantified it in a new and useful way.

We've all heard the expression, "practice makes perfect", but even in my youth I heard coaches correct this version by saying, "no... *perfect* practice makes perfect."

This fits with an often-overlooked part of Gladwell's thesis, which is the practice needs to be directed, *intentional practice* as opposed to idly strumming a guitar or swinging a golf club. Rather, it's about intentionally and willfully working on improving certain aspects of whatever craft you aim to master. This might involve the assistance of a capable teacher, a good how-to manual or YouTube series, or focused and creative trial-and-error. Whatever the method, one by one, areas targeted for improvement should be honed until they are mastered.

A good example might be someone wanting to master their golf game. They might first analyze where they are losing strokes relative to par to see where they can get the most benefit through correction. They might find they are losing a ton of strokes due to poor tee shots, and bad putting (most commonly) and might start off working on those areas. That might involve analyzing what they are doing wrong (perhaps with the help of a teaching pro and video analysis), getting some instruction on how to correct their errors, and repeatedly practicing correct technique until the frequency of faults gets to an acceptable level. You might go through a similar iterative process to master the piano, or writing or sculpting.

This all seems pretty logical but as Gladwell emphasizes, the focus must be on *intentional practice*, or working at something rather than playing at it. It involves being focused and working in a directed way toward a goal (though hopefully, if you're doing something you love, it doesn't feel like work).

Gladwell also quantifies the intentional practice at roughly 10,000 hours (which might vary depending on the complexity of the subject). While one might quibble about the exact number, the important take-away here is that it's clearly is not a matter of a few weeks, nor is it a lifetime. Looking at 10,000 hours, if someone invested 20 hours a week, they could put in 10,000 hours over ten years. Or if they put in 40 hours per week, they could do it in five years.

And this progression does not vary based on a person's level of natural-born talent. Even "prodigies" don't get to skip the steps. Mozart began composing concertos around the age of ten, but he didn't compose what would be considered his first masterwork until he was 21 – mastery took him eleven years. Again, with this process we're talking about mastery of a craft rather than innate talent. Clearly, Mozart had both going for him.

The Beatles is another example cited by Gladwell. In 1960, before anyone had heard of them, an agent booked them for an extended gig in a strip club in Hamburg, Germany. The gig didn't pay well and the patrons weren't paying attention to the music, but it was a paying gig and they were required to play eight-hour sets, seven days a week.

Over the next few years, the group played more than 1,200 live performances in Hamburg, exceeding 10,000 hours, more than most bands would play live in a lifetime. Not only did this commitment force them to play together a lot, it also forced them to broaden their repertoire to include a wide range of music and some original compositions. It also helped them learn to live together as a team, which served to knit them together for another ten years.

As Beatles' biographer Philip Norman claims: "So by the time they returned to England from Hamburg, Germany, they sounded like no one else. It was the making of them."

Clearly the Beatles were an example of talent meeting intentional practice. The Hamburg gig is a little understood facet of the development of what would become the "overnight sensation" of The Beatles.

In reading various histories of classic rock bands, I've been struck by the number of stories that follow a common theme. A kid hears Elvis Presley for the first time, flips out, says "That's what I want to do!", then gets an old guitar or drum kit, and five years later, bursts onto the scene as a rock star at the age of 19 or so. I've particularly marveled at stories about kids that pick up a guitar at 14 and are able to play it at a world-class level just five years later. Obviously, the answer is five years and 10,000 hours of obsessive, goal-oriented, intentional practice...and some lucky breaks.

Upon reading *Outliers*, I realized I had experienced the phenomenon (in a small way) a few times. In my late 20's, I started doing crosswords with the goal of being able to complete the puzzles in the *New York Times*. However, that's a tough place to start, so I began doing what I could do each day of the *Times'* puzzle (not much), then also doing a few more of lesser difficulty. I typically worked four puzzles a day. I would further the intentional part by studying the answer keys so I could learn. I did this religiously until I could complete the *Times'* puzzle on a regular basis.

I wouldn't say I'm a world-class crossword solver (I thought I was good until I saw the elite competitions in the movie "Wordplay!"), but I know I've mastered the craft. And it seemed like a natural process where (a) I developed an interest, (b) I decided I wanted to be really good at it, (c) I set a goal, and (d) I worked at it with a plan...except it didn't feel like work.

I did this as well with another hobby I picked up in the late '90's, when I started collecting bobblehead dolls from the 1960's – papier-mache nodders that were made in Japan.

These pieces were delicate, and tended to get damaged in various ways. At first, I sent my damaged nodders to a master repairer I'd heard about. But being fairly handy, I started to do some repairs on my own – experimenting and making up my own techniques and finding the best materials for me. I got to the point where my work was fairly presentable. And then one day I got word that the master had died, and I realized I was probably as good as any repairer out there.

I began doing repairs for other people and developed a reputation. Over the years, I've repaired somewhere between 4,000 to 5,000 pieces, accumulating a good multiple of 10,000 hours. When I look back, I realize I was always looking for ways to improve the quality of my work and to work more efficiently – and that focus continues to this day. There's no doubt that I had a very intentional attitude toward improving my craft. One might argue this is a silly hobby and an even sillier thing to crow about, but this is my art and I'm proud for having developed some mastery in it.

We know "Practice makes perfect" is more accurately stated as, "Perfect practice makes perfect". Whether you buy Gladwell's theoretical time estimate of 10,000 hours, the real message is that anyone of average ability or intelligence can aspire to master a craft, sport or activity, and with sufficient, focused and intentional practice, can indeed master it – which is a most hopeful notion for all of us.

What's 10,000 hours when you're talking about developing skills for a passion you can enjoy for a lifetime?

> "If people knew how hard I worked to get my mastery, it wouldn't seem so wonderful at all."
> - Michelangelo

14

Four Stages of Learning
a New Task

When you are beginning any sort of new undertaking, there is always some sort of learning curve involved where the more you do it, the more capable you become. This applies to anything new, whether a job role or task of any kind, maybe a new dance routine, a music piece, or even a new relationship.

No matter how much you want to hit the ground running and be a star from Day 1, it's a virtual impossibility and nobody in their right mind should expect that from you. This is a good thing to know, and acknowledge, so you can be realistic and not put undue pressure on yourself (Don't worry!).

Specifically, there are four necessary and progressive stages everyone goes through in learning any new task, skill or routine. There is no skipping steps. This applies to cases of Mastery in 10,000 Hours or a relatively simple task. You will necessarily go through each stage and you never recognize where you are in this progression at any given moment...you will only see it in hindsight.

Once I became aware of this, I have recognized it in everything I've done, from new jobs, to coaching to bobblehead repair (the jury is still out on parenting – somehow you never quite know where you are with that one). And it can be enlightening to look back and witness it.

Getting started with the stages:

Stage 1: Unconsciously Incompetent – You might start out with the idea that you know something about what you're embarking on because you've done a similar job, or know something about it, or have been educated for this, or have played a piece of music like it. But the fact is, you *don't* really know it and nothing has quite prepared you for this particular challenge at this particular moment. So, you really aren't capable of doing this yet, but you're not aware of that fact. This is not to say that you don't have the capability, but you don't have a mastery of all you will need to succeed. To coin a phrase, "You don't know what you don't know" – you're not aware of the pieces you will need to master for success. Thus, you are "unconsciously incompetent" for the task. But don't worry, there is hope ahead.

Stage 2: Consciously Incompetent – You will have charged into the new task with your energy and a blind sense of faux competence, and you will run into roadblocks. Situations will arise that will make you aware of what you are not prepared for. You've never run into this before, you've never seen an environment like this, people are different, or it's just not what you expected. In short, your head is spinning. And you wonder: Why did I start this? What made me think I could do this? Will I ever get a grip on this before people discover what a putz I am?

As the possibility of failure enters your mind, panic sets in. Instead, you need to relax (granted, this is easy to do in hindsight!). Recognizing the gap between your actual capability and the mastery required in this new task is a good and healthy next step. And once you've done it, you can work on closing the gap. Recognition is the first step in solving the problem. You've become consciously aware of your relative incompetence at the new task, at least for the moment. But there's always tomorrow...

Stage 3: Unconsciously Competent – Having recognized the gaps in your mastery of the new task – your current level of incompetency – you have set out some points to work on. These might be building new areas or techniques into your knowledge base, relationships/contacts that need to be developed, or whatever you decide is missing. You need some new tools in your bag or a better grip on your environment. You will work to fill in these gaps and show people that maybe you are well-suited for this after all. Having panicked about the possibility of failure in Stage 2, all your attention is focused on scurrying to fix this and prove you can do it. And with so much of your attention fixated on the panic and perceived shortcomings, you don't realize the gaps are getting closed, you're starting to get it, and become competent. Yet your focus is still on the shortfalls of Stage 2...so at this juncture, you're unaware of the fact but you've actually become unconsciously competent.

Stage 4: Consciously Competent – Then one day you wake up and you say, "I can do this!" or, even better "I got this!" You realize you've got a handle on the job/task/new dance routine and you're good to go. You recognize that the gaps have been filled, your work has paid off, and you're now confident that you are succeeding. Your little bit of panic may have been overdone but it served to rally your efforts. You may even feel like, "nobody can do this like I can." All the better. You were already getting to the point of competence in Stage 3, but your awareness of the fact had not caught up to the reality. Once you become aware, i.e., consciously competent, you can begin to own that competence and proceed with confidence. What's more, you can appreciate the journey as you look back at the four stages.

I've said that everyone goes through these four stages in adapting to a new task. I will, however, offer a caveat or two. The Four Stages assume a level of introspection and some sense of reality. People who travel through life somewhat mindlessly – as we said, the ones who say, "what happened?" – are unlikely to question their fit for a new task or recognize any shortfalls in their capability. But anyone who does (honestly) self-assess along the way will necessarily and naturally proceed through this four-stage process.

I can't emphasize enough the importance of those two qualifiers: introspection and being real/honest. As we face any situation, we want to honestly be aware of our own role with respect to environment, our capabilities and responsibility. This requires a level of humility and integrity, two invaluable qualities that will also serve you well in all that you do.

You might consider this four-stage construct to be an overly-analytical approach to a fairly simple, organic process. I think of it as an interesting way to look at what we go through as we enter any new realm. It can also be entertaining to consider in the rear-view mirror – the only way you can see it at all. But more than anything, I think you'll find it to be a hopeful and reassuring way to look at the challenges you will face as you embark on any new task or role.

> "If someone offers you an amazing opportunity and you're not sure you can do it, say yes...then learn how to do it later."
>
> – *Richard Branson*

15

Don't Focus on the Prize

Once again, I've given instruction with the negative "Don't." And once again, I've done it for a reason, because people so commonly focus on the M-O-N-E-Y (or other reward) that it becomes the all-encompassing target.

Let me put it this way: If you want to stay poor, then by all means focus on the money (or maybe the prize, the reward, or the accolades).

On the other hand, if you would like to reap the rewards that come from success, focus on the *doing*. Put your attention on your craft, or your work or your creative pursuits. If you're following your passion and bringing all your talents toward that effort, the results will follow, and the rewards will most likely be beyond your expectations. I have experienced this for myself.

As a college student I was a scholarship football player and a serious engineering student who viewed the "scholar-athlete" concept as the ideal – I wanted to succeed and see how far I could go in both realms. I was doing what I wanted to do, following my passion for sports, and I was having fun at it all. I knew I could hack it academically but wasn't sure if I ever would in football. I worked and trained and bulked up in the hopes of seeing time on the field. By the end of my sophomore season, I was able to start the last few games, and then keep the job the next year. I was aware there was such a thing as the Academic-All American team, and one night walking to my dorm after practice, it occurred to me that *that* is the ultimate of the ideal...it surely was well beyond my grasp, but that is the ideal. No one had ever been so honored at Villanova, and I didn't have the nerve to even dream it – a fleeting thought and then I forgot about it.

Then, following my junior season, no one was more shocked than I to learn that I'd been named to the Division 1 Academic-All American Team (2nd team), which I then repeated as a senior as well. I had had this crazy vision on a solitary walk of an ideal that to my mind was completely unrealistic...it was a fanciful and fleeting thought which I never would mention to anyone. But I had a direction and I just put my head down and did every bit of work I knew how to do in order to max myself out, both in the classroom and on the field....and the rewards turned out to be well beyond anything I could have realistically imagined. And all because I was focused on doing what I could do to get on the field, and then doing my job, rather than any reward.

Focus on the doing. Think about it this way: If a good tennis coach wants a player to serve aces, she doesn't tell her pupil to serve aces or even to visualize serving aces. What could any player possibly do with that instruction? Instead, she will give her pupil the tools to serve aces. This will involve the proper mechanics, focus and mindset, as well as practice to create muscle memory. The approach is to teach and practice the best techniques that lead to the desired outcome, so the results will then follow.

To look at another scenario, let's say you would like to get married at some point, or maybe just want to find a significant other.

Would you, (a) look for someone attractive to you and then focus on proposing marriage (or an exclusive relationship)? Or would you, (b) start to get to know the person, find out what makes them happy, and see if you share common values and a common vision for the relationship? I think most people would go with (b).

The (a) option focuses on the desired outcome and the rewards. The (b) option focuses on the factors that tend to lead to a positive outcome. If done properly, with the right party, there's a much better chance of a successful result. Put another way, one option is ridiculous; one makes some sense. This is the difference between focusing on the money or the rewards versus focusing on the doing.

For another view of this, consider a baseball pitcher: He will work on the proper mechanics to execute all his pitches, hone his mental skills, and develop a game plan for each batter. Yet when game time comes and the pitcher executes – releasing the ball – the result is literally out of his hands. There are any number of possible outcomes depending on the batter, the fielders, the umpire, and so on. Looking at the bigger picture over the course of those games, these individual outcomes add up to wins and losses and a season's worth of statistics.

If the pitcher is playing for his next contract (based on his statistical results) and maybe an award, it is pointless for him to focus on the contract or the award, or even wins and losses. The only piece of this equation that he has any control over is the part where he preps for a game and then executes each pitch. The same goes for any effort that involves a team or interaction with other elements. All any of us can do is to focus on the doing, worry about the part we control, and then trust the results.

Or as we often hear today, "Trust the *process*, not the results."

Another important point: As you consider entering into a new undertaking, whether a career change, starting a business, getting involved in a social cause or committing to a relationship, it's important to ask a fundamental question: *Why am I doing this?*

Think of this question as your Mission Statement. In teaching business strategy, I tell my students that this is a clear and necessary step, a way to lay out a company's reason for being, its *raison d'etre*. Another way of putting it might be: What difference do we want to make with this company? This could involve identifying a problem that people commonly have and solving it with the company's product. For a safety product, that might mean reducing accidents. Or something to make peoples' lives easier, or free up their time, or help them connect with like-minded people, (i.e., as with eBay or match.com).

The same goes for a cause-related effort – the Mission Statement should lay out the problem the effort hopes to address, such as homelessness, food shortages, social injustice, or access to healthcare. But the basic question, again, is what difference do we want to make with this effort? What do we want to change? What do we stand for?

This mission-statement-thinking even applies to committing to a relationship. Perhaps the mission might be to have children and raise them to be responsible role models and contributors to the world beyond your lifetime.

Any good effort should have a definable and positive mission, one that stands up to some level of scrutiny in the light of day. Of course, for some founders, the real mission is M-O-N-E-Y, regardless of what they wrote in their Mission Statement to raise capital. These businesses will have a harder time reaching that success than the businesses that stand for a strong sense of mission. There are two reasons why I say this:

1. That founder will always be a servant to the money rather than focusing on serving any sort of client – whether a user, a cause, or a need to be filled. Any sense of a reason-for-being will always take a backseat to money goals. "The doing" is subsumed by the possible rewards.
2. If a cause is worthwhile and the mission is compelling, people will sign up or invest. This goes for potential employees, customers, as well as investors, all of whom are necessary to success. If the mission is phony, people will avoid or abandon it.

Any time you embark on an effort, it makes sense to think in terms of mission. If this is a career, maybe you want to be around an industry or activity you are passionate about. Maybe you're consumed by music but not a talented enough musician to be a professional artist. Yet you dream of working for a music label, or representing artists, or being a recording engineer. Your real interest – your mission – is to be working within the music industry... and that's fine.

Or let's say you are a musical performer who is actually talented enough to do it professionally. You may start out thinking in terms of being able to do what you love and pay your bills, or have an album recorded. But at some point, you may aspire to a higher purpose. You may have a different sound in mind that you want to create. Or you may want to cause people to feel something – an emotion – when they listen to your music. Ultimately, you may want to create something that will endure beyond your time on earth. I've heard some artists speak in such terms. As in this example, it's very understandable and okay to keep your mission within reach for where you stand at a given time, then readjust later as your situation and your skills change.

By thinking in terms of mission and asking yourself questions such as *What difference do I want to make?* or *Why am I doing this?*, you will begin to focus more naturally on the doing, rather than on the rewards. Those who succeed beyond their hopes and dreams tend to be people who focus on solving a problem and making a difference, and often, they end up being celebrated for their achievements.

And don't be dissuaded by what may seem like an enormity of challenges and time that will likely be involved in your mission. A Chinese proverb says, "A journey of a thousand miles begins with a single step." That is, even the longest and most difficult undertakings have a starting point, which is the first step, then the next and the next. Keep your eye on that first step, not on the entirety of the challenges involved in the journey, or else you'll be overwhelmed and more apt to give up before you begin. If all you see are the obstacles, then that becomes an obstacle in itself, and it will immobilize you.

But by putting one foot in front of the other, step by step, you will soon be on your way. This brings to mind the earlier "Don't worry" shortcut, where we talked about not borrowing tomorrow's troubles when today has troubles enough on its own. What we can control is right in front of us...the first step...the pitcher throwing the next pitch. Keep your focus on doing the specific actions that lead to the successful goal that you're seeking, and then the results – and rewards – will likely be beyond your expectations.

> "You don't get results by focusing on results. You get results by focusing on the actions that produce results."
>
> - *Mike Hawkins*

16

Don't Sweat the Small Stuff (Hint: It's All Small Stuff)

How many decisions do you make in a day? If you count every little choice, they're likely innumerable. Most are innocuous little decisions you're barely aware of, like which socks to put on. Maybe there are a handful that cause you to consciously consider your options and make an overt choice, like how to handle an important task at work or how to dress for an appointment. Of the latter group, how many of these decisions might cause you to sweat a little, leading you to pore over the options and weigh the pluses and minuses in a mental Ben Franklin-style chart?

I don't know about you but I might go through a couple of these per day. And my message to you is to just not worry about them. Because the vast majority of these decisions will not appreciably affect your life (nor anyone else's) in the long run. So, as author Richard Carlson put it:

> Rule #1: Don't Sweat the Small Stuff
> Rule #2: It's All Small Stuff

I admit, I don't always follow those rules. I might sweat over what to order for lunch – do I want the Caprese Salad, or maybe the BLT? I might wonder which one they make better here. And I might consider what I will be having for dinner. In the moment, it can feel as if there is so much riding on this decision. And why am I sweating over it? By tomorrow, chances are I won't even remember what I ate. Honestly, we get ourselves fixated over the silliest things.

For perspective, I would guess that there are only a handful of decisions you will make in a *lifetime* that will truly be meaningful at the end of the day – ones where, looking back, you would say that they really changed the course of your life. Maybe it's a dozen decisions at most. But you can bet that none of those include what you ordered for lunch.

Now, if you're a perfectionist and you want everything to be just so, and you want to be comforted in the knowledge that you're making all correct decisions, I have three points for you:

1. Get over yourself and loosen up. Nobody makes perfect decisions all the time and no one should expect to. In fact, have a laugh at yourself over some of your goofier decisions.
2. Why do you need to be so exacting when it comes to the small stuff? Why not use these ordinary instances to take some chances. Go crazy and order the Caesar Salad with Grilled Chicken!
3. The French philosopher Voltaire said, "The perfect is the enemy of the good," meaning that for most decisions and efforts, "good" is good enough. Aiming for perfection can get you to a point of diminishing returns and wasted time and attention. In fact, it's easy to ruin something that is perfectly good as you continue to pursue it toward perfection. While perfection is a noble ideal, the cost of getting

there is usually prohibitive when you have a perfectly good situation in hand.

I know this territory well. I want to be a perfectionist, and as such I need to remind myself of these points all the time.

If you are a person who is prone to anxiety over decisions, these rules are meant for you. I hope you'll take some comfort in knowing that the stakes involved with most of your decisions are quite low, so you should proceed without worry. To put this in some perspective: What is the difference between walking a foot-wide plank on the ground versus that same plank spanning two ten-story buildings? Only the stakes. Take away the fear of falling ten stories and they're the same task. But, one you would do on a $5 bet, and the other, not so much. The vast majority of daily decisions are the plank on the ground.

If, on the other hand, you are less a perfectionist but rather tend toward being a slacker, maybe "It's all small stuff" is the last thing you need to hear. Maybe you need to ratchet up the attention level a bit and skip this shortcut. Or...maybe the slacker has something to teach us all. You decide.

One final note to lower the pressure involved with even big decisions: Another of my favorite sayings: *"The successful person is not the one who makes all right decisions, but the one who makes their decisions right"*. That is, the outcomes for most decisions tend to play out over a period of time. This means that on most occasions – even for a big decision – you still have a chance to influence the outcome after the decision is made, through your own efforts and persistence.

One example I've experienced has to do with my selection of colleges – perhaps one of those decisions that might actually change the course of your life in various ways. Sparing you the details, suffice it to say that I had one idea and my dad had a different one. On this (rare) occasion, I dug in my heels and stuck to my guns. He finally conceded but left me with a message that would stay with me – knowing that I had a top Ivy League in mind for grad school and not believing that my college choice was a good avenue to get there, he told me, "Well, just make sure to create a good enough record so you can get into the graduate school of your choice."

I was motivated enough on my own to reach my goal, but if I ever wavered, his second-guessing would often ring in my ears as a reminder of what I was after. I became very focused and diligent through my undergrad years, succeeded in my scholar-athlete pursuits, and made it to Harvard.

In other words, I proceeded to *make* my decision the right one by focusing on the doing, and not letting anything distract me from putting together a great overall college resume. For anyone who is armed with conviction about a decision, this is a common occurrence – to be committed to a decision and then endeavor to prove that it's the correct one...that is, to make the decision right.

Aside from decisions, interpersonal situations and how we're per-ceived by others are areas that might sometimes seem to take on outsized importance. Most of us are overly sensitized to our feared mistakes or social faux pas. But unless you have a stalker, it's a good bet that nobody is paying that much attention to every-thing you do. I grew my first beard this year and...nobody noticed (not even my wife!). The world is not paying so much attention to what you're wearing, doing or saying. Generally, they're worrying about their own issues. This is good news. At the end of the day, most stuff is inconsequential. So let yourself relax.

Realizing this is one of the luxuries that comes with getting older. You realize that things – decisions, actions, situations – that you once fretted about no longer matter. In fact, virtually everything that happened last week has little impact today. (And certainly not that Greek salad you finally ordered for lunch, after so much internal debate.) Isn't that comforting?

> "If you treat every situation as a life and death matter, you'll die a lot of times."
> *- Dean Smith, former NCAA Coach*

17

Are You Looking for Solutions or Excuses?

When talking about success – whatever your definition or your pursuit – it's all about attitude, right? Let's break that down a bit and understand the implications of that.

The mindset that you bring to any situation is crucial to the potential outcome. Yes, attitude makes a difference, and the outcome can almost be preordained before you even begin...based on your outlook and commitment.

Some people look at every challenge as an opportunity...every problem, every job, every encounter. For these folks, even receiving an angry call from a customer could be a chance to provide superior service and create a loyal customer for life. Every misunderstanding with a friend can be an opportunity to have a meaningful discussion and develop a stronger relationship. It takes an extraordinary attitude but some people can even see opportunity for growth in a car accident or other trauma.

And then there are people who see only problems.

Which group do you want to be in? Do you want to look for solutions or excuses?

When I use the word *attitude*, I'm not referring to the overt signs of a "positive" or a "negative" attitude. I'm talking about an outlook that lies deeper within you. It's something you need to ask yourself with honesty, since few people would openly admit they are looking for excuses, even to themselves. What I'm talking about is almost more subconscious.

If you're looking for solutions, you enter into a situation with a mindset of looking to fix the problem, solve the puzzle, or build something. Your focus is only on solving the problem – "there must be a way" – rather than on the downside of failure. Even as you encounter the inevitable obstacles, you again focus on opportunity, with a mindset that there must be a solution here.

When a person is looking for excuses, on the other hand, you can hear it in subtle ways when they discuss a problem. Maybe they're looking for why their efforts will fail, anticipating the pitfalls or a negative reaction to the effort; maybe they're looking for a thousand reasons not to embark on the effort at all.

Since anyone undertaking any project is likely to encounter obstacles along the way, these are basically escape hatches to make an early getaway. The person looking for excuses has already built in a justification for why the effort is doomed – "The design won't work" or "Nobody will buy that." The new obstacle then becomes the rationale to hit the button for the escape hatch. This person's effort is doomed before it starts. Yet this person is often unaware that this is their plan, but it's baked into the attitude they bring to the effort.

John Madden, the former NFL football coach and announcer liked to fire people up with an expression, to "load up the wagons and burn the bridges." To my mind it refers to going into battle and taking the fight to the enemy across the river – meaning it's essential to load up everything you've got, cross the bridge, then burn the bridges behind you. You're committed. It's a fight to the death with no option of retreat (i.e., no escape hatch).

I'm not sure Madden's listeners understood what he meant (though I'm sure they appreciated his colorful style) but the imagery nails the difference between looking for solutions versus excuses. It speaks to making a commitment to being successful, fighting to win, or (metaphorically) die trying. This is obviously a dire way to look at an undertaking (especially a football game) but it gets the point across. How committed are you toward your idea or effort?

I enjoy watching the television show Shark Tank, where aspiring entrepreneurs pitch their startup business ideas to the "Shark" investors. Among the great qualifiers the Sharks look for is the commitment demonstrated by the entrepreneurs. They love it when the person has given up a good, well-paying career and/or invested their savings or borrowed serious money, thus demonstrating their great belief in their venture. They've loaded up the wagons and burned the bridges. On the other hand, the Sharks tend to be skeptical if a person is doing their venture as a side gig while keeping their day job. In those cases, they'll either decline to invest, or, if they really love the idea, they might invest with the condition of replacing the entrepreneur. But the message is that they're looking for the positive, solution-seeking, die-trying attitude, and gauging it by the demonstrated level of commitment.

Of course, most of us are in between the extremes of always problem-solving and excuse-seeking, hovering between the two attitudes. What's important is that you listen to yourself – listen to your self-talk and pay attention to how you couch your thinking. If you recognize that there will be obstacles but they can be overcome, that sounds like a healthy attitude and a good way to move forward. But if all you can see is the obstacles, then, (a) perhaps you can recognize this might not be for you, and may not be something to pursue, or (b) if it's something you really want, you'll want to consciously adjust your attitude before embarking on the effort, remind yourself that every effort comes with obstacles, and avoid undermining yourself before you get started. You don't necessarily need to identify all the obstacles at the outset – and you may not have all the solutions – but you need an attitude that there is nothing that can't be overcome.

One other aspect of attitude to consider is the role of procrastination. We all procrastinate when a task seems monumental or has an uncertain outcome. I tend to be pretty obsessive when it comes to performing simple routine tasks like paying bills or replying to emails. But if it's a bigger, longer-range project, I'll be the first one to drag my feet, wondering, do I really want to do this, or maybe I can start it tomorrow? In this regard, there is a wonderful quote which seems to derive from Jewish wisdom, attributed to Andrew Toynbee:

> "If it's to be, it's up to me" ...to which I would add:
> And if not now, then when?

If something is important enough in your life, it's up to you to do something about it. Nothing happens until you take the first step. Once again, "A journey of a thousand miles begins with a single step." Or... How do you eat an elephant? One bite at a time. You just have to make a decision, and then dive in. And, conversely, not making a decision (procrastination) *is* a decision.

If I hadn't reflected on Toynbee's comment – and in particular my addition, "And if not now, then when?" – I might have never gotten around to writing this book. In the face of a big writing project, and with COVID restrictions, one day blended into the rest, making it easier than usual to procrastinate forever. Instead, on the day

I had the idea, I made a do-able plan where I vowed to write-up a new topic every weekday until I had a first draft. And I followed that plan, one bite at a time. This is how projects get done.

It also would have been easy to get bogged down in considering the obstacles I would face in writing a book – that is, the *excuses* for why I shouldn't proceed. For starters, what did I know about commercially producing a book? And most obviously, how can you sell a book in the "Personal Growth" category without either a marketable name or at least a professional Psych credential? Instead I decided this was a book I needed to write and a project I needed to do, regardless of typical marketability factors. And I would find the *solutions* – I'd learn what I needed and find the resources to produce a book. And then I'd do the same for marketing it.

We know that attitude makes all the difference...not only in your outcomes but also with your happiness in life. This could apply to a job, a project, an idea, a relationship or anything. Be honest with yourself and ask, are you looking for solutions or excuses?

> "We have more ability than willpower, and it is often an excuse to ourselves that we imagine that things are impossible."
> - *Francois De La Rochefoucauld*

18

You Can't Do It All on Your Own

Whether you consider yourself a rugged individualist or, on the other extreme, a person who is fairly dependent on others, the same message applies: You can't do it all on your own. Asking for help is not a sign of weakness; on the contrary, you'll likely be amazed by how many people are happy to lend a hand.

I'm all for independence and self-reliance; they are wonderful traits to develop and I recommend them highly. And while it's not wrong to look to yourself as you take on a new task, and say, "I can do it myself," no one knows it all, especially when we're entering new territory. There might be a need for new information, new contacts, or any sort of support, including financial backing, guidance, or complementary skills. Or maybe just additional hands to help. Reaching out for what you need is a sign of good judgement; it signals that you understand your limitations or the need to leverage your skills.

Admittedly, my first inclination tends to be to do things myself, whether it's a matter of business or home repair. ("Why call someone when I can do it myself?") A few reasons for my (and other people's) reluctance include:

1. *Pride: You don't want to admit you have limitations.* Which brings to mind the phrase from the Book of Proverbs: "Pride goeth before a fall," not to mention the quip every one of us heard from our grade school teachers: "There is no such thing as a stupid question." Indeed, half of the class probably has the very same question, so get over your reluctance to ask.

2. *You're afraid your request for help will be turned down.* That is certainly a possibility, but that denial usually has more to do with the other person's busy-ness or personality than it does with you. Generally, people are willing and happy to help, especially if you make the request easy on them – for example, maybe you can do some homework ahead of time and tee up the requested issue for them, so maybe they only need to make a call or provide some advice. It also helps to be sincere, and to show appreciation. Everybody has needed help at one time or another, and appreciated someone's assistance, and you might be amazed how some people will go out of their way to help, often unexpectedly.

3. *You don't want to bother someone.* You might be surprised to know that people often like an opportunity to "pay it forward", as someone might have once helped them. Or they might be flattered to be looked to for expertise or guidance. Everyone likes to feel needed, even if it means taking some time out of their day to offer assistance.

4. *You don't want to be indebted.* First of all, what's wrong with owing someone a favor, especially if their favor ends up helping you along? Secondly, not everyone thinks about things in such a transactional manner. They might simply be happy to help, especially if they are in a more senior or mentor-type position relative to you. I would also argue that having "a debt" of sorts can be a good thing. This creates a dialog or an excuse to carry on a conversation

– and ongoing relationships can be forged when "one hand washes the other."

When we're talking about seeking out specific expertise or contacts, another way of asking for help, there is nothing like the power of networking. I initially hated the idea of networking – to me, it sounded like a cheesy, multi-level-marketing scam. I told myself I would never be comfortable reaching out to people I didn't know. But the fact is that, (a) we all need to do it (everyone can use a hand), (b) it's not cheesy; it's a well-accepted and useful practice, and (c) it *can* be uncomfortable, until you have some success with it, in which case it can become an interesting (and maybe even fun) practice. Not least, you're operating with one hand tied behind your back if you don't do it.

I've used networking when I've been looking to go in new directions, whether looking for a job or not. The first step is to develop a list of people who might have some knowledge in the area that you're focusing on. Start with people you know, then turn to people with whom you might share an implied bond. For instance, plucking out names from a college alumni directory is fair game; strangers will often take a call or an email from a fellow alum of State U. If you let yourself be imaginative, you'll be amazed at the people you can reach, if again, you make it easy for them, you are earnest, and show knowledge and appreciation. I've even cold-called well-known retired people and had amazing chats by following this simple formula.

The best approach to networking is to avoid appearing to be in a position of desperation. You may be looking for a job, but as you reach out to people, you don't need to say your goal is to get a job. Rather, your goal should be to gain insight and contacts in your field of interest. People don't want to be put in the position of having to tell you they don't have a job for you, and they won't want to refer you to one of their contacts for them to tell you that either. The intention should truly be to learn what you can about the field, how people get started in it, what realistic paths might be and that sort of thing. If you demonstrate some good interest, willingness to learn, and curiosity, be assured that they'll let you know if they've heard of a job opening. Networking goes easier if you're not putting anyone into a potentially difficult spot.

It helps, too, to always finish a conversation – whether in a meeting or on Zoom or via email – by asking if there is anyone else they know who might be willing to speak to you. If they offer to put you in contact with other people directly, great, but it's also fine if you can use the name of the person you just spoke with when reaching out to their contacts. And, as always, make it easy on that person, too.

One thing to keep in mind when you're networking is that your immediate goal is simply... the networking (with the conversations and opportunities to learn along the way). In computer networking lingo, you need to think of everyone as a node (connection point) rather than as an end point. Your goal with every contact is to make more and more contacts and spread the network, rather than getting to your ultimate goal. It helps to make a game out of it. And again, believe me, if you're making good contacts and following the advice discussed above, people will let you know if there is something they can specifically do for you. Otherwise, proceed on to acquiring more contacts.

As you move along in this process, you will find that some people you had great hopes for may disappoint you. These cases may reveal something about the nature of the relationship you have with those people, or, once again, it could have to do with someone being busy, or some other unrelated factor. Then again, complete strangers may take up your cause and go above and beyond. In this case, you will be gratified to enjoy the kindness of strangers. And you will remember these experiences later when someone looks to you for assistance. Remember, too, not to pre-judge or assume that someone does or doesn't know about the subject you're exploring. You can never predict what some people know (or don't know).

Along with looking at networking as a bit of a game, it can also become an interesting study of human behavior if you let it. For example, I found that for all my fear of cold-calling strangers, most people wound up being much more accepting of the outreach than I imagined. And some strangers will go above and beyond to help, somewhat adopting your cause and asking you to keep them apprised of your progress. And meanwhile others from whom you might have anticipated help may not bother to assist. This is all part of the process. One plus: You'll find that the more you do it, the easier and more natural it will become; you'll also become expert in what works and what doesn't work for you.

I've been describing networking in a job seeking context, but it can also be used within organizations, neighborhoods, communities, or fields of interest. It can start with a chance meeting and a casual conversation – start a conversation and there is a possibility; when you avoid that conversation, there are no possibilities.

So, whether you're just asking for directions, or help with a problem, or you're taking it to a next step with networking, don't be afraid to ask for help. Nobody can do it all on their own (and why would you want to?).

"I get by with a little help from my friends."
- John Lennon

19

-- -- -- -- -- -- -- -- --

The Personal Touch

You have a lot invested in you – that is, everything is riding on being the unique and special person that you are. Why hide that when you're out in the world trying to get things done?

This is a strong appeal for you to bring your persona and your presence to bear in every way you can as you operate and navigate your way through life. The world needs you and your unique contributions, and you deserve to put your best foot forward.

What craziness am I talking about here? Essentially, I'm saying never to miss a chance to use the personal touch in all of your interactions.

The more we connect electronically, the easier it is to lose the personal touch. It's easier and more efficient to text someone than to get them on the phone; it's easier to talk on the phone rather than meet someone in person, and so on. But so much subtlety and context can be lost in a text, breeding misunderstandings. Efficiency is great, but it's not efficient if you need to go back and fix a misunderstanding that could have been avoided.

The fact is, all of us are more *effective* in every way by being present and in front of someone (including Zoom or on the phone), whatever we are trying to do. Maybe you're applying for a job, or recruiting someone, or trying to convince someone (or just reaching out to an old friend). I always feel I have a fighting chance if I can sit in front of someone and state my case. With a personal appeal, they can see the sincerity in your eyes. And it's harder to say "no" directly to a person (even when they're on a screen) than it is by text. We all have the personal power to be persuasive, so don't fail to use it when you need it.

We talked previously about networking in the old school way of truly making contacts. Of course, there are all sorts of online and social media techniques for networking such as LinkedIn. Those sources may be a vehicle to obtain names but any online networking will be enhanced by bringing a personal touch to bear. It not only distinguishes you from the crowd but also demonstrates a level of effort and earnestness that will be appreciated.

Any expression of humanity and contact qualifies for what I'm calling "the personal touch." Instead of mailing something that you promised someone, if you can, drop it off; you may run into the person and have a conversation. When someone has given you some time or done something for you, thank you notes are also a wonderful thing (email is good, but don't forget handwritten thank-you's). They are becoming increasingly rare, which means you really stand out when you send them.

There is a place for the Internet and social media, too, of course. If you will be interacting with someone new, go online and try to learn what you can about them. You may discover that you have a common interest which can always be helpful in forming a connection. Connectedness is really what we're talking about with the personal touch.

And let's not forget about your personal relationships with friends, family, and maybe a significant other. The more of a personal touch you can bring, the healthier and more satisfying your connections will be. Don't miss a chance to acknowledge an acquaintance's little victory. Reach out if you haven't been in contact. We never know when a simple "hello" or an innocuous suggestion may make a difference for someone we care about.

As our world becomes more focused on skills – technical training, analytics, AI – it's easy to lose sight of the fact that the world is about people (until AI takes over). People make the decisions. You get things done with people and through people. And people need people; we all need human contact.

After having been trained in business and then been out in the business world, I sometimes wonder if I should have studied the humanities or psychology; in some ways, it's a better preparation for a career in business than an MBA. Most of business is a great deal of common sense and logic. But understanding different people, human motivations, and how organizations work as social bodies is really what makes a difference. And effectively communicating as well. This applies to any field whether it is a business, a cause, politics, or any sort of grouping. At the end of the day, it's all about people.

So, at a time when the world is in dire need of more humanity and more socialization, one thing you can do to make a difference is to bring your personal touch to bear. There is an entire spectrum of levels, from online to in-person meeting, with many steps in-between. And while there are times when a text is perfectly effective and unobtrusive, if you're trying to make an impression, build a relationship, or make some sort of appeal, try something a little further up the touch-level chain. I've had some great successes with chance, drive-by deliveries. There is nothing lost in the effort, and there might be something great gained.

Until the machines take over, people still make the world go 'round; life is about people. Right now, especially, the world needs you and the humanity you can bring to keep it livable. You owe it to yourself to put your best foot forward and bring your unique personal touch to all that you do. When you do, you'll be the most effective version of yourself and make the greatest possible contribution.

> "I've learned that people will forget what you said, people will forget what you did, but people will never forget how you made them feel."
>   - *Maya Angelou*

20

On-The-Job Training

Growing up, I wasn't schooled in the real world; nobody told me that life was hard or that it wasn't fair. I was brought up to believe it was a meritocracy out there, that if I did the right things (e.g., worked hard, met my deadlines), and avoided doing the wrong things (e.g., getting in trouble, not being truthful), I would succeed. None of this prepared me for life in the real world. There was a lot I needed to learn about what to expect in the world.

I also assumed adults in various positions of responsibility and authority knew what they were doing, whether businesspeople, politicians, teachers or coaches. Because, if life was a meritocracy, then people in positions of power must have demonstrated some level of competence to get there. Wrong again.

My first job after grad school, in particular, was a real eye-opener. The gig was at a Fortune 300 company that happened to have just been named one of the *Forbes'* Five Best Managed Companies. But it didn't take long before I recognized the organizational dys-function around me, as well as varying levels of competence. As I mentioned earlier, I was stunned that I could stand out by merely doing the basics of my job.

I tell you this not to dump on corporations but to (a) set proper expectations, and (b) offer a message of hope. And just to be clear, what I discovered applies not just to corporations but all sorts of organizations in our daily lives. While there are clearly some that are better than others, it's fair to assume that excellence isn't necessarily the norm.

In truth, the whole world is getting by with on-the-job training. Not many people really know their job thoroughly – these days, few people stay in a job long enough to get to know it fully, and organizations generally don't have the luxury of training and coaching their people. In my day, managers tended to have up to seven direct reports (the widely-followed "Rule of 7" claimed you couldn't effectively manage more than seven people at a time), but today, it's common for managers to be responsible for more than twice that number. Organizations have gotten leaner management-wise, and with that change, individual coaching has largely gone by the wayside.

Moreover, in today's dynamic organization, if a person is in the same job for a year, they've hit a dead end. So not only do people rarely get a chance to become competent, but they don't stick around long enough to be accountable for the results of their decisions, which adds to the organization's dysfunction.

And this has nothing to do with people's overall ability...in fact today's workplace entrants are better prepared overall than ever. To the contrary, nobody wants to be poor at what they do... they're smart enough, they're trying to do their job well, and want to contribute. As we mentioned, these are more often failures of management to train and coach properly; in turn, these managers are often under pressure from senior management to "run lean", so staff development is relegated to being an unaffordable luxury.

Once, I felt a bit intimidated to go into a new job where I would be "unconsciously incompetent," but I came to realize that is the norm. Nobody is really expecting you to know your new job and everyone is faking it while learning on-the-job (including your boss). So try not be overwhelmed at the prospect of moving into a new role of any kind – someone saw enough in you to recommend you. But chances are that you, too, will be learning via on-the-job training, left to your own devices to figure things out. That's when you need to use some of the tools I've talked about here, starting with the need to think, be curious, and take initiative to learn about your role. Ask co-workers for help. Build bridges with people from other departments. Try the "personal touch" to glean knowledge and talk to lots of people.

All this talk about challenged organizations may sound like a gross generalization and unduly harsh. But if you enter a situation with low-ish expectations, you will not be disappointed. More than anything, though, you shouldn't be intimidated as you go into new situations – you are there for a reason, you will apply yourself and go through a learning curve, and you will most likely exceed everyone's expectations.

> "I hear and I forget.
> I see and I remember.
> I do and I understand."
>
> - Confucius

21

Someone Has to Lead

Leadership is a favorite subject of mine. I find it fascinating to see the range of approaches that can be effective, with the one constant being that any effective approach needs to be an honest expression of who the leader is.

In any organization, someone has to lead. Though two people can work collaboratively as partners, when you add a third person, someone has to lead, to set a direction and sort out any differences that ultimately arise.

Even the Japanese, who make decisions within groups through consensus, deliberating until they arrive at a point of being of a single mind – when you look closer, you see that the group discussion continues in a coordinated Kabuki-dance sort of process until the group jointly arrives at the leader's preferred option. Even in such a collaborative environment, where everyone feels involved, effective decision-making only happens through leadership. Every grouping needs a leader.

I like the expression "Either lead, follow, or get out of the way." It's a little cold, but it expresses the truism that effective groups need leaders, and they certainly need followers. What they don't need are people who undermine the group's effort.

Leadership is a much-studied topic with volumes upon volumes devoted to it so I won't delve too deeply here. But I think people tend to follow someone who looks like they know where they're going. It may have to do with a vision for how things should be, or it may just be a display of confidence in one's ability to figure things out. In the best situations, followers are drawn to those qualities in a leader and the leader has legitimately earned a fol-lowership, rather than when someone is artificially thrust into a position of authority.

We don't hear a lot about followership. But if a leader doesn't have good, constructive followers, there's no one to do the work. A good follower can also act as a counter-balance or sounding board – no single person, even the leader, should make all the decisions or come up with all the ideas. Leaders should be good listeners and directors of the process. Good followers should also keep leaders accountable to the group – call them out when they are not listening or getting too bossy, or maybe not living up to the group's mission. Good follower-ship is an underrated role vital to any group.

Generally, all of us gravitate toward one or the other of these roles, depending on the situation. We hold out leadership roles as a very positive thing in our society, but it can be a lot of work and responsibility to lead, and some people may be more com-fortable as a team member or follower. That doesn't mean they won't want to lead when it comes to something very important to them, or if they know the subject thoroughly. Personally, I can be comfortable in either role, unless I don't have confidence in a potential leader, in which case I'd much rather be the leader than be part of an ineffectual group.

You may not think of yourself as a leader, or think you're not comfortable raising your hand to lead. I was that kid in grade school. I never thought to run for class office or any such thing. I had a 4th grade teacher, Ms. Siegel, who was a wonderful teacher and also led the school's Safety Patrol – these were student patrols stationed at all the street crossings near the school, sporting a badge on a belt across their shoulder. To my mind, this was a real nerd operation, and a responsibility with no upside.

Then, one day late in my 4th grade year, Ms. Siegel asked if I would do her a favor and be a substitute patrol for a month. I loved Ms. Siegel and couldn't say no, even if this might ruin my rep (as if I had a rep). At the end of the month, I got Patrol-of-the-Month, and I liked that (I guess she understood who was starved for recognition, and I responded well to it). We came back for 5th grade, and somehow now I was Captain of the Safety Patrol (a.k.a., Head Nerd). With the blue captain's badge came responsibilities, but it also had its bennies. For example, since I did the scheduling, I could make my schedule work for me. Very clever, that Ms. Siegel, I guess she knew her boy well. I was hooked, and leadership became a comfortable and positive role for me from that point on.

I was cultivated and selected for leadership of the Safety Patrol – a common way to determine a leader. But this doesn't always happen within groups – sometimes in class or at work, people are selected to work as a group and sent off to figure it out. Even in a study group that forms for school, someone still needs to lead, to direct the work or just to schedule meeting times.

Selecting a leader might be a matter of a vote, or as simple as someone raising their hand with no one objecting. But it can be awkward as you ponder whether you want to be that person. Maybe raising your hand makes you feel pushy. Maybe you're not sure you want the responsibility.

Recently, I had a Zoom call with a large group of fellow alums who tend to be pretty accomplished, and we had breakout groups to work on various topics. As soon as the breakout began, there was a dead silence. Everyone on the call was a leader-type, but no one wanted to pull rank or step on anyone's toes by assuming a leader role. Someone finally broke the ice and we all fell into follower roles, understanding that anyone could lead this, that we were all mature and it was okay to just get on with it. But I found it to be a funny and instructive group dynamic.

Suffice it to say, being a leader and being a follower are both good and necessary roles for effective groups. Both have their own responsibilities. And being a good follower – or perhaps better termed as a "team member" – is an underestimated and vital role. I recommend both roles, at various times. But once you get a group of three or more, *someone* has to lead. And so, sometimes, why not you?

> "Someone needs to lead, and someone needs to follow, but they are both equally on the same team."
> *- Mark Naird, as played by*
> *Steve Carell in "Space Force"*

Part III
Quality of Life

22

-- -- -- -- -- -- -- -- -- -- --

Planning is Overrated

As someone who has developed business plans for a living, and as a business professor who was trained in planning skills, I should probably not be telling you this, but I promised to give you the truth: Planning is overrated.

This pertains to any sort of planning such as career planning, business planning, or life planning. As we said earlier, "People plan, and God Laughs." Whether you believe in God or not, the idea that you can say with certainty what you will do tomorrow is laughable. You might have a plan, but what happens if you wake up and your car won't start? Or you have a severe cold? Or someone close to you has died? Or the power is out? There are a million situations that can change your priorities for the day, rendering that plan useless.

Mike Tyson was a heavyweight boxing champ who was particularly scary – he was referred to as the "Baddest Dude on the Planet." When he was asked whether he was worried about his opponent's fight plan, Tyson replied, "Everybody has a plan until they get punched in the mouth." This quote reminds me of another old truism used in combat as well as in business: "No battle plan survives first contact with the enemy."

Don't get me wrong – it's good to have a plan, and even better if the plan has contingencies built in. But once the action begins, all bets are off. You may encounter something that you never imagined. Your opponent (or possibly "life") may deal you something totally uncharacteristic or unforeseen, at which time you will need to scramble until you can devise a new plan. A boxing match, or a battle, or a business competing for customers provide good examples of this idea, but it could just as well pertain to your career, or your personal finances, or anything else you might plan.

Plans can even have negative effects if not used properly. In my first job, my company had an elaborate financial planning process that would drive the business for the coming year. The problem was that when unforeseen situations would arise (as they always do) – when they got "punched in the mouth" – they were too rigid in their thinking and too afraid to disappoint Wall Street analysts. The forecast numbers were sacred and needed to be met, no matter what.

As a result, as a young Sales Manager, I was under pressure to participate in illegal accounting tricks (falsified sales) in order to "make the numbers." I was able to avoid doing that but some of my peers did take part in activity that was illegal, unethical and bad business from every angle. The point is that being a slave to your plan can be self-defeating, and lead you to places you don't want to go.

Before Dwight Eisenhower was President, he was an Army General who, as Supreme Commander of the Allied Forces in Europe for WWII, led the elaborate D-Day Invasion plan and eventually won the war in Europe. Sounds like someone who would believe in plans. However, his quote on the subject – while at first sounding nonsensical – hits the nail on the head: "Plans are nothing; planning is everything."

In other words, the plan itself is virtually useless once it is created. It will certainly meet up with an action from the enemy (in battle) and then you will need to respond appropriately. However, the *process* of planning causes you to think through alternative courses, studying the costs and benefits of various approaches, so that when you need to act, you've already done your homework. And you can respond quickly.

Similarly, business plans should be used for their proper uses, with the understanding they have their limitations. They should be created as a tool to gauge whether you have a business or not. That is, how quickly you can reasonably expect to grow the sales of the business, the cost to deliver what you say you will, whether there will be any profit left over, and how much capital will be needed to get to that profitability. If the plan is done credibly and it looks attractive, you might be able to convince a financier to invest in the business. But that is about all that should be expected from the business plan. It should not be looked at as a promise or even an expectation for what will occur. I've never seen a business plan that accurately predicted the future.

How does this pertain to you? To sleep well at night, we all want to know our future will be secure, and our life will proceed in a favorable way. We want to follow our passion and become successful on our chosen path. So we often plan out the steps that lead in that direction, getting the requisite schooling, the experience, etc. The same thing may pertain to your personal life in terms of where you decide to live, or when you might hope to marry.

And then life occurs. Maybe a punch in the mouth? Or maybe something altogether different and more fantastic. Remember, I said the business plan (or battle plan) is partially based on certain expectations or assumptions? That's true, but when you get there, the situation may be totally different, negatively or positively. Maybe the economy has tanked. Or the competition pre-empted you with a better product. Or maybe your progress (on your business or your career track) has far exceeded your expectations and now you should be setting your sights higher. The plan is just a plan; but the planning process can help you decide if this is a road you want to travel and how you might get there.

I love the way these two quotes get deeper into the nature of planning, in different ways.

> "A goal without a plan is just a wish."
> - Antoine de Saint-Exupery

> "Without leaps of imagination or dreaming, we lose the excitement of possibilities. Dreaming, after all, is a form of planning."
> - Gloria Steinem

At first glance, you may wonder, *Which is it?* Are goals just wishes in the absence of a plan, or are wishes and dreams an important part of planning? The answer (of course) is "both." As you consider what you want (your goals), you need to think through how you might get there, what might be required, and whether that is realistic for you. On the other hand, you need to have a dream, some sort of vision of what happiness might look like for you. Just because you can't see that outcome from where you are sitting right now doesn't mean you can't dream about it and think about how you might get there.

There are actually two very different approaches to planning. There is "forward-planning," as I described in the business-planning process. That involves taking the things you know today and what you expect to do, then factoring in assumptions about the future to see where it goes.

The other approach is sometimes referred to as "backward-planning," where you set a goal, then work backward from there to devise a plan. This is often used in education and training, but also in business planning. This can be a very powerful tool to go beyond what you are able to see, and think about very visionary solutions that don't currently exist. You start out thinking about an amazing product or a dream-like outcome, and then track backward, imagining the potential hurdles and possible solutions required to ultimately pull it off. This is how great visionaries start out when creating their breakthrough innovations.

You can do the same with your life. Certainly we all do this with our career choices, e.g., we might decide on a profession such as the Law. The first obvious steps in the rites of entry would be to go to law school and pass the bar exam. However if you further aspired to sit on the Supreme Court, you might study the current members to look for patterns of experiences that played a role in ascending to the Supreme Court, including elite law schools and certain important clerkships. And networking with influential players in the system.

You might also think about where you want to wind up in life and work backwards. For example, you might want to have a loving family and grandkids. You might want to be known for furthering a cause or solving a societal issue. Maybe you want to be known for having created something. Or possibly you just want to be known as someone who was a leader in their community and treated everyone well. Whatever the goal, you can look to that vision and work backwards for a path that might lead you there.

Whether you do it backwards or forwards, keep your plan in the proper perspective. A plan is not a recipe in a cookbook, where if you follow the steps correctly, you'll wind up with a cake. A plan is also not a contract, where you are guaranteed a certain outcome. Planning is good as part of a *process*. Planning gets you thinking about how to get from here to there – hopefully in a realistic way – and with the room to make adjustments as situations change.

This all begs the question: If planning is overrated, how do we get to that happy place, however you define it, especially if you don't even know if your chosen path is the right one for you?

I was always a person who wanted to go to sleep secure in the knowledge that I had an idea of where I was going, with an actual plan in place. Now, I can tell you with certainty that the more of life I experience and observe, the more I discover that getting to a "right" place tends to be a combination of the following ideas we've discussed elsewhere:

- Luck, or the randomness of life
- Chance encounters (and being vigilant for them)
- Good timing
- Preparedness and learning
- Being open, with a readiness to act
- Being honest with your heart

Things happen for reasons that we can't even fathom...good things and bad things. And though most of us want to control our lives, and our outcomes (and often foolishly believe we can do this) no one can say for certain that a minute from now the Wi-Fi won't go down or that a stranger won't offer the opportunity of a lifetime. So while it's good to go through the process of planning, don't stress out over it – remember, planning is overrated.

> "Life is what happens to you while you're busy making other plans."
>   - John Lennon, from "Beautiful Boy"

23

-- -- -- -- -- -- -- -- -- -- -- -- --

Embrace the Journey

As a culture, we Americans are exceptionally goal-oriented. One reason is that for someone with high aspirations, there are so many opportunities here that it encourages goal-seeking. No surprise, then, that we tend to focus on the goal rather than the journey. But as we discussed earlier, the goal is actually more attainable if you direct your energies toward the doing rather than toward the reward itself.

So why are we always in a hurry to get somewhere, to get that errand done, or to graduate, or to reach a level in our career, or to be married? The fact is, very few of the routes leading to your goals will follow any sort of smooth path. If you were to plot your progress toward these goals on a graph versus time, you'd likely get an erratic, saw-tooth line...hopefully trending upward (but not always). There may be periods with virtually no progress, followed by a major leap, and then a possible setback. And then, maybe, arriving at the goal, or even overshooting it.

My life has been a perfect example of this - a series of very irregular progressions, with lulls of dissatisfaction followed by an embracing of new possibilities. With respect to my career, I started out very

productively, on a soaring path, hit various bumps in the road...
and then spent too many years figuring out what was not working
before moving on to much more satisfying pursuits. I delayed a
number of years in marrying the woman I loved, and could have
missed out on it. My overall happiness has been like a roller coaster
of emotions. These have all been very irregular progressions.

Most of the time, we're not in the midst of achieving any of our
goals anyway. The vast majority of our time is spent in one of
those highs or lows on that saw-tooth progress chart. That progress chart is our journey.

So if we're fixated only on the goal, then we're spending most of
our time frustrated. *Why haven't I gotten there yet? I'm falling behind my peers. I need to get to this goal so I can set my sights on the
next one. What's wrong with me that I'm not getting there?* I spent a
number of years with those frustrations.

This line of thinking is perfectly natural, but it is so wrong on so
many counts:

- Once again, focusing on the reward is the hardest way to
  get to the reward. In fact, it might even assure that you
  never get there.
- This is an unrealistic way to view progress toward an as-
  piration. Progress tends to proceed not on a smooth path
  but rather in fits and starts.
- Comparing your progress with that of others is like comparing a chicken to a spaceship – there is no relevant basis
  for comparison. We all have our own paths to follow, our
  own baggage to deal with, our own list of considerations,
  and our own abilities.
- If you're focused only on the goal, you're missing most of
  the show. The vast majority of your time is spent on the
  way to the goal. So instead of being mired in frustration at

your relative lack of progress along the way, *embrace the journey* and *enjoy the show.*

There are all sorts of opportunities that can pop up while we are on that path toward our goal(s)...there are many roses to smell, many beautiful sunsets, countless surprises, setbacks, recoveries, challenges, things overcome. They should all be appreciated as part of the process.

Sometimes I get myself off the goal obsession by adopting a salesperson mentality: "I'm going to be cold-calling strangers all day. Statistically, I know I'm only likely to make one sale for every 20 cold-calls, so for every rejection, I smile and say thank you because I'm one call closer to the 20th." That's smelling the roses. That's recognizing that it's all a process, and embracing the journey.

How do we embrace the journey?

1. Focus on the little victories. There will be small steps as you progress toward your goal. Celebrate those, appreciate the progress, and chalk one up in the "win column." Never fail to take the opportunity to celebrate a little win for the home team.
2. Be grateful for the good things in your life. We tend to get so caught up in the setbacks or the negative aspects in our lives. Sometimes, we need to consciously focus on all the pluses we have going for us – the things we should appreciate. As I say, you just never know if today isn't as good as it will get. Things can change, and what you don't appreciate today may not even be there tomorrow. COVID has reminded us of that with the loss of the freedom to mingle, enjoy good health, or the health of a loved one... things we might have taken for granted that we are now truly starting to appreciate.

3. Learn from the experience. As we're on that jagged path to our goal, remember that it's not all positive steps and little victories. There are also missteps. These don't have to be negative, unless we fail to learn from them. Like that salesperson, you can say, "Thank you, this brings me a step closer to my goal".

4. Try new things. We all become creatures of habit; human beings embrace routine. "That routine got me this far." But if you're stuck somewhere in your journey, don't be afraid to try new things. I did that when I felt stuck in my life and my then-fiancé suggested the possibility of psychotherapy. I tried it out thinking I'd only do it for a short time to work out some career issues, but stayed for a number of years because it worked for all facets of my life. The alternative is to keep trying the same thing while expecting a different result...as we know, the definition of insanity.

5. Value the people you meet along the way. Sometimes, we're so focused on our goals that we fail to recognize how our life is enhanced by the experience...especially the people we meet, who help us, or become friends, or who are just different and interesting. Some people spend a lifetime collecting friends – that's a nice way to go.

All of life is a process, the small steps and the overarching process that lead to your living a good and fulfilling life. That salesperson getting to the 20th call (and getting a "yes" in the process). Getting your degrees. Getting a job. Getting to work each day. Making a marriage work. Embrace the journey and smell the roses.

Another way to look at it is: Your Story, as in, What is Your Story going to say?

A major tenet of Hinduism is the concept of reincarnation, where the soul is eternal and repeatedly returns to the physical world in a new body. Each time the soul is learning new things, to reach higher levels of consciousness and to work through its karma until it reaches the highest level of consciousness. You come back at the level where you left off, and you keep coming back until you get it right. It's a nice concept. Maybe that's the deal, and if so, what do you need to learn in this life? What trials do you need to go through? At the end of the day, what's your story going to say?

"Sometimes you win, sometimes you learn."
- *John C. Maxwell*

24

- - - - - - - - - - -

Paris or Vienna?

This topic begins with a woman, who is a mother of an autistic child. The mother is reading a story about a woman who has spent her life dreaming of traveling to Paris. She has read tales of Paris, full of beauty and magic, and she is sure Paris is her dream place. She imagines maybe she was even switched at birth and she should have actually grown up in Paris. And she is certain that if she ever gets there, her life will also be wonderful and full of magic.

So, she spends years saving her money and planning for the day when she can travel to Paris. Preparations made, she finally books a flight to Paris, which she awaits with great anticipation.

The day arrives and she couldn't be more excited. She boards the airplane and gets settled in. But as the flight is taking off and the pilot makes the announcement for the flight, he announces the destination is Vienna. The woman is crushed and has no idea what happened, but she is now on the Vienna flight and there is no turning back. She couldn't be more disappointed.

Yet when she arrives in Vienna, it's springtime, the weather is perfect, there are flowers and birds chirping, and everywhere she goes there is music and laughter. She starts to explore Vienna and realizes there is beauty like she never imagined. And she decides that maybe Vienna is the place for her after all.

Back to the woman reading the story. When she reads this tale, she breaks down in tears as she realizes it parallels her own experience. Like all parents, she had dreamed of having a healthy child who would not face difficult life challenges. But her child is autistic. Yet despite that, she realizes that for all the love she gives her child, she feels that love returned many times over. And every bit of progress that her child has made has been incredibly gratifying. She didn't know what having an unchallenged child was like. She only knew she couldn't imagine experiencing such love with another child.

She thought she wanted Paris, but she had no idea of the joy and beauty that she might find in Vienna.

I must tell you, this story was very meaningful for me with regards to my own overall happiness. I had imagined that my career would take me to some high-ranking corporate executive position – that maybe I'd be responsible for building something pretty great, and I believed this would be gratifying. And when that didn't happen, I was disappointed – in myself and (probably) in the world. Then later, I had transitioned into doing some consulting, using what I had learned, and also functioning as the house-dad and community volunteer.

Looking back (and upon reading this tale), I realized I had never really gotten much satisfaction or fulfillment out of my business experience – even in positions where I had been successful, I didn't believe what I had accomplished had made much of a difference. Meanwhile, with a daughter in high school and well on her way, I realized that I wouldn't have traded the time I'd spent with her during her formative years for anything in the world. I had gotten far more love, sense of purpose, and fulfillment from that than anything I'd done in business. What's more, the community involvement allowed me to meet some wonderful friends, and the coaching experience was surprisingly gratifying, which then led to a gig in teaching...which led to this book.

My idea of my own Paris turned out to be an ill-fitting and doomed destination, for me at least. Clearly, I had dreamed of Paris but found Vienna to be just right for me.

This realization had a wonderful effect on my outlook and my happiness. I no longer needed to feel disappointed in myself for not fulfilling my dream. I just needed to feel fortunate I didn't miss the plane to Vienna and to appreciate it had worked out the way it had.

We all have hopes and dreams. We all have some ideas – whether explicit or in general terms – of how we imagine our life will go. This might include achieving some lofty place in our chosen field, making a difference in the world (however we define that), having a family, realizing some level of monetary success or comfort, or exploring something. Or it might just be a blanket goal of being happy throughout life.

In our fantasies, we never dream of hitting obstacles. We never dream of things not going well. We don't dream about becoming ill...or having a loved-one become ill. Or having an accident. Or about money challenges causing a change in plans. When we fantasize about how we want our life to go, we don't dwell on all the things that happen that might derail a dream or a plan.

Derek Jeter is the legendary former Yankees' shortstop who wrote a book entitled, *The Life You Imagine: Life Lessons for Achieving Your Dreams*. The Amazon description starts with, "Ever wonder what it would take to turn all of your dreams into reality? In *The Life You Imagine*, All-Star New York Yankees shortstop Derek Jeter shows how you can use the same game plan that helped an eight-year-old boy who fantasized about playing baseball for the Bronx Bombers grow up and become MVP of the 2000 World Series."

Jeter wrote this book at the age of 26. Initially my reaction was to say, Wow, this guy did a school assignment at age 8 about becoming the Yankees' shortstop, which he details in the book. But the more I live and the more I observe of the world, my reaction is...good for him, but he's got a lot of life left ahead of him. And while there are people who seem to lead charmed lives, I'm not sure how much there is to be learned from their experiences. For most of us, Derek Jeter's story is pretty much a fairy tale. It may be as wonderful as it appears, but his is not a common experience, regardless of your game plan.

As I mentioned, for most of us, life happens, occurrences out of our control, miscalculations made, poor health, accidents, a global recession. All kinds of reversals, most out of our control.

It's the way we respond to these challenges that makes all the difference. I don't know too many people who are totally living out their dreams as they imagined them. At some point, life occurs, and you might be served up a detour...a gate change between the Paris and Vienna flights.

And at the juncture where you realize you're in Vienna, look for the beauty and joy in Vienna. Don't lament the fact that you missed Paris...or resent the circumstances that led you to Vienna. You might point to other people, or responsibilities, or fates, or some supernatural force, or yourself, as the reason you wound up in Vienna. But the fact is, you're in Vienna, and maybe there's a good reason why.

It may well be that your Paris is not the right fit for you, as it wasn't for me – which is why I found it to be so tough to get there. I wasn't always able to acknowledge that. I believe that for me to recognize my own Vienna, it had to be so different than my dream – and for so many good and gratifying things to occur – in order for me to be able to grasp it. That, and a little nudge from reading the story of Paris or Vienna...and I also had to be ready to hear that message.

There can be all kinds of reasons why you might not want to – or be able to – recognize Vienna. If your dream is a powerful one, you likely have a lot wrapped up in that; it may be part of who you are. There might be ego involved, and stubbornness. And there might be outside pressures to live up to the Paris story – expectations of parents, or peers, or partners. We've got a lot riding on Paris. I hope it lives up to its billing...but if it doesn't happen, look for your Vienna.

By all means, chase your dreams, shoot for Paris, there's nothing wrong with Paris. As we said earlier, follow your passions. And don't be deterred – there will be challenges and obstacles, which will make your journey and your ultimate success more rewarding. Go after it, and keep going.

But somewhere along the journey, if you realize you're off on a different path than you imagined...that new path could be immediately wonderful, or it could appear to be a real comedown from the path you imagined. Either way, keep in mind the story of Paris and Vienna, and be open to the idea that Vienna just might be your dream place.

> "Maybe the journey isn't so much about becoming anything. Maybe it's about un-becoming everything that isn't really you so you can become who you were meant to be in the first place."
> - *Paulo Coelho*

25

Maybe Your Most
Important Decision Ever

At great risk here, I'm going to wade into potentially controversial territory, not because I love danger but because I promised to be real, and because this "shortcut" is too important to avoid.

I mentioned earlier that there are probably only a handful or so of your life's decisions that, when you are drawing your last gasp, you would say were seminal points in the course of your life. A different decision may have led your life in a very different direction. The subjects of these decisions may vary from person to person. The choice of a college may or may not be on the list. Or it could be a decision to move somewhere which put you in position for many great outcomes.

For me, the decision that has made the largest impact on my life was my choice of a life partner. It not only set the course for the person I would share my journey with, but also determined who I would have a family with and share in the stewardship of that family. To a fair degree, maybe you could even say it helped determine *what kind of person* I was going to be. This is a decision that is devilish if you don't get it right, but when you do, it's the best thing in the world.

Now, the tricky part of this topic. The form of relationships is an evolving phenomenon in our society. The what, how, and who may change over your lifetime. Marriage rates are declining. Nothing is a given. As such, I am not going to espouse the traditional approach to marriage as the right choice for everyone. What I will say is, activities you commit to and stick with tend to be more rewarding than things you just dabble in.

My marriage would certainly be considered a very traditional one, but our roles have been very non-traditional. This was not by design but rather evolved out of practicality. There was a point when our daughter was an infant when I was not employed and my wife had just begun a promising new job. Since we had options, we decided I would stay home and do any work activities from there.

As I've described, this led to a series of experiences for me that were totally unexpected and rewarding. I was most fortunate to have a wife and partner who was willing to take on what became her role as the "primary breadwinner," while I took on the more day-to-day role of parenting and otherwise making a life for us in the community. More than anything, I had a most rewarding firsthand experience seeing our daughter grow and mature, which also changed me for the better. The point is that my wife and I have always viewed ourselves as a team, and we will share duties as needed – this is the sort of partnership that works. The result was not necessarily what I envisioned, but you also need to remain flexible since there is no way to know what circumstances await you. And it may turn out that you don't really know what might be best for you (i.e., your "Vienna").

The point is, the person you choose for a mate might very well be the most important decision you make. You're already going to spend the rest of your life with yourself, and your mate might be the only other person who also does that. Who you choose for a mate will affect your happiness, hopefully keep you more balanced – with concern for another person – and will enter into other large decisions, as you take your partner's interests into account. I am not a relationship counselor or a family therapist. I'm just a guy who has been married for 24 years and who has observed what works and what seems to not work very well (in our relationship and in many others'). Advice is tricky, but I will propose some thoughts for consideration, understanding that they come from a fairly traditional perspective:

> **Timing** The right time is very individual. And even if the timing feels right, you need to meet the right person. Which means multiple factors need to come together. But who's to say that you're really ready, versus you've met someone you're excited about, so you only think you're ready? Only you can answer that.

> I know I was not ready until I was at least 40. Before then, I was not mature enough and I was still carrying around too much baggage about the kind of person I "should" marry. It also wasn't until 40 that I could fully let someone into my life, and make the decision based on what would truly make me happy. I also decided I wanted to commit to the relationship whether or not we could have children. Realistically that was going to be very challenging at our age of 42. As it turned out, we were very fortunate. Most people get to this point much earlier and don't necessarily have this as a consideration. My journey was different.

The important thing is to be mature enough to truly let another person into your life and secure enough in your understanding of the traits that will work for you in the long run. You also have to be at a point of being able to make decisions with your own happiness in mind, rather than that of an outside party. Only you can know when you've reached that point and when you have met the right person.

Values This may be the most underrated factor in a relationship that lasts, especially if children enter the equation. There needs to be a mesh of values such as honesty, integrity, ideas around money, how your alliance will operate, and, in the event you have children, how you might raise them. When you have children especially, it's most important that parents agree on the values they want to instill in their offspring.

As Antoine de Saint-Exupery said, "Love is not just looking at each other, it's looking in the same direction." If two people are not aligned in their values, sooner or later a situation will arise that will expose their different priorities. And it will be a source of strife. This is another reason why maturity is so important; you need to truly understand your own values.

Friendship At the end of the day, you hope that your mate can be your best friend or maybe I should say "best mate." That is, someone who understands you perhaps better than you understand yourself. Someone who likes you the way you are. Someone who is in tune with what's going on in your head. Someone who nurtures and refreshes you. And just as importantly, someone where it feels easy to do all these things for them as well.

When we think of love, most of us imagine fireworks going off, and I believe those fireworks are important, though they can mean different things to different people. There has to be something intangible in that person that you don't want to be without – let's say it's just a feeling. The fireworks may or may not last, but you hope that at a minimum your mate can be your best friend; one that you can hang with forever. That's something that can last. And sharing a sunrise together can bring more than twice the pleasure of watching it alone.

Respect This is another of those make-or-break factors. Any couple who shares a happy life together must have mutual respect for each other. They think of each other as equals, neither one more important, neither dominating decision-making, neither getting more than they're giving, neither making more effort than the other. Over time, if these kinds of things are not relatively in balance, the relationship won't work. I've seen many relationships fall apart when there is a power imbalance and associated imbalance of respect. I've never seen a good long-term partnership of any type that didn't include good mutual respect.

All of these points – and I'll stop with those – could just as well apply to other significant relationships in your life, with a close friend or a business partner. We all have various other priorities on our list. It could be a certain look, or a sense of humor, or shared interests. That's up to you to decide, and again, to some degree we figure that out when we meet the right one. As we learned earlier, we make those decisions in the limbic area of our brain...and then we debate the logic in the reasoning area of the brain, to justify what the emotional part wants to do. If that sounds complicated, don't worry – you'll know when the time and person are right.

These are just some ideas from a person who believes in the value of a long-term committed relationship as an important piece of long-term happiness. Another way to approach this topic is to look at a couple whose relationship you admire, and to think about what you believe they have going for them.

What I wish for everyone is that they might find their own form of happiness, whatever that is. Life offers infinite opportunities for things to experience. Marriage or some form of life partnership – and possibly raising a family – are but two of those, and can be profoundly rewarding. You can't fully experience these things by merely being a close observer. You need to be in it, and you need to be all in.

And it might be the most important decision you make.

> "My husband has made me laugh. Wiped my tears. Hugged me tight. Watched me succeed. Seen me fail. Kept me strong. My husband is a promise that I will have a friend forever."
>
> *- Unknown*

26

It's OK to Choose
Your Own Family

I know this sounds like heresy but hear me out on this.

Many of us are raised hearing that "Nothing is more important than family." This is a concept that is passed along from generation to generation, and I agree that the bond with family can be like no other. There are shared experiences, there is a feeling of mutual protection, and a sense of loyalty among family that many of us carry for a lifetime. The expression "Blood is thicker than water" came about for a reason.

However nobody has ever updated the definition of "family." The traditional notion is based on the idea of the "nuclear family" – a social unit consisting of two parents and their children. Any observer of modern society would immediately recognize that this is a somewhat outdated concept that is divorced from common practice and not very inclusive of a wide variety of family situations.

For starters, how does a person draw the boundaries on their "family" in cases of adoption? And might the answer be different if the transition takes place at birth versus at age 10? In the case of divorce and remarriages, how do multiple step-families fit the model? Today, there are any number of family situations that don't easily fit into the notion of the nuclear family, in which case, how do you define "family"?

So right off the bat, there are structural questions to ask when someone says, "Nothing is more important than family." And then, what if you come from a very narrow family tree? I came from a large paternal family, but my mom was the last person in her family line. Similarly, my wife comes from parents who were only children, and she has one sister. If family really is the most important thing, a person like my wife could be made to feel poor in the sense of family.

And what if your family experience is actually a source of pain? What if your family is very dysfunctional, or abusive? Should you feel obligated to hold your family in such regard if it actually has had a negative effect on your emotional well-being? That sounds like a recipe for feelings of obligation and guilt, and more pain.

So while I do believe family is a wonderful thing and can be a great source of strength and nourishment, that's not always the case. And when it's not the case, it's okay for you to choose your own family. Yes, once again, you get to choose.

At one point I had a sports blog, and I wrote one post where I raised the idea that it's okay to declare yourself a free-agent fan. This, too, was considered heresy. What I meant is that rather than being stuck in an "abusive relationship" as a fan of a franchise that is badly run and (because of family ownership) might be bad for generations, you can think about declaring yourself a free agent and switching to a more deserving team. When I talk about family,

I'm suggesting you might consider having such an option in a similar way, if need be.

There's another expression I like: "There are friends, there is family, and then there are friends that become family." You could define your family circle in any way that you choose. It could include lifelong friends. It could include a neighbor, or a childhood mentor who was like a parent.

As I've described, my grandfather was uneducated but he was very wise – and he used to brag (with tongue-in-cheek) that he was a "very rich man." Financially, at best you could say he was comfortable...but what he meant was "rich in blood." My grandparents created a large and loving family, and he truly was rich in family, in every way.

I feel that way as well. Yes, I am part of that same family legacy with my brothers and a sister, cousins, aunts and uncles...and of course, my wife and daughter. I too feel very rich in blood. But I also feel rich in friends. I have strong circles of friends from high school, college, and grad school, where we talk regularly and get together when possible. And in later years I have made some great friends in our community that provide further enjoyment. When I think about it, these people are part of what I consider to be my family. And I feel like a "very rich man" too.

It's true that friends will come and go in your life. But the best ones will be with you for life – "like family". I've also observed that it's easier to make friends in school, and more broadly when you're younger. You're more likely to be able to have crazy bonding experiences and just have fun together when you're young. As you get older, while you'd think your world would get broader, in fact, for most of us the world tends to get a bit narrower as you define what you like and don't like, what you'll put up with or not. As such, the friends you make later in life might be closer to your way of thinking than any of your old friends, though they just don't have that "history." But it all makes for a good, well-rounded family.

So yes, "family is the most important thing." But you can define family as you see fit. Make sure your biological family is what you need...that it gives you comfort, provides pleasure, refreshes you, and nurtures you. And you can add to that family with friends. And regardless, it's okay to also define *family* as it works for you.

> "If there ever comes a day when we can't be to-
> gether, keep me in your heart. I'll be there forever."
> *- Winnie the Pooh (A.A. Milne)*

27

--- --- --- --- --- --- --- --- ---

Doing the Right Thing

No lecturing or moralizing here. Ethics is a subject where we will not delve too far into the substance of ethical behavior, and the importance for each of us to create our own system of ethics. To me, it is a private subject that is first informed by our upbringing, and then becomes a matter of choice as we make decisions for our own lives.

But I think it's safe to say that most of us, day to day, try to do the right things. In fact, I often remind myself of this when I get frustrated with a person or situation...that everyone is trying their best, however they're equipped. And I don't mean this in a condescending way by any means, but merely to make allowances for people being imperfect. If someone disappoints you, or is insensitive to you, or annoys you, it probably has less to do with you than it does with whatever is going on in their life.

So, while striving not to lecture on what anyone's ethics should be (and who's to say what the "right thing" is anyway?), it's important to consider a few brief points.

First, be aware of your own values, what *you* think is right or wrong, what you are willing to do and what lines you won't cross. As Alexander Hamilton said, "If you don't stand for something, you'll fall for anything." You want to think about what works for you, which will typically be a mixture of values you observed growing up combined with experiences you've had throughout life, as well as what *feels* right or doesn't. The point is to be aware that you have your own system of ethics, to own it, and to live it.

The second point has to do with setting your ethical expectations. I had a business professor who passed this along for use as we embarked on our careers, but the advice is just as valid for other areas of life. He told us we should start out with our ethical standards set at a high level, and fight like heck to maintain them to that level as well as we can. That's because over time that standard can only go in one direction, and that is down. It's not as if you can scam your way to a fortune with the idea that you'll make your pile, turn over a new leaf, and then live a virtuous life; it just doesn't work that way. Once you've strayed, there's typically no going back.

On the other hand, even as you consciously try to maintain a high ethical standard, over time you will be faced with temptations to cut corners to get ahead or to acquire something. And you may be faced with conflicting pressures that cause you to compromise. That's real life, and we're all human. So start out with high ideals and a good ethical standard, then fight to keep it there, because it may only erode over time.

Earlier, I mentioned the ethical dilemma I faced as a young Sales Manager pressured to falsify customer sales invoices to inflate our reported financial results. Before this came about, I remember reading a news story about another computer company that had been caught doing this on a major scale, and it caused the demise of that company. And I remember thinking, "How dumb could these people be to get caught up in something like that?"

A year later, I found myself in that sort of position myself. I was able to resist participating because my sales numbers were pretty good and I wasn't worried about losing my job. But I saw my peers do it, some to curry favor with the bosses, or maybe try to play the hero. The level of this fraud would increase quarter to quarter until it was getting to be a significant number. And I thought to myself, "I guess that's how people can be dumb enough to get caught up in a scam like that." The point is, once you tell a lie, it's easier to tell the next lie, and then the next. And at some point, you've become a liar.

I've often reflected back on my professor's prescient comments from 40 years ago. As for your own ethical standard: be aware of it, own it, set your sight high and try like heck to keep it there.

"Relativity applies to physics, not ethics."
- Albert Einstein

28

What's the Rush?

In one of his video interviews, author/thought leader Simon Sinek talks about his interactions with young people in the working world. When he asks one how her first job is going, she says, "I think I'm going to leave." He says, "Oh no. You just started nine months ago, you loved it." She replies, "I just don't think I'm making a difference."

I hear this sort of scenario repeated, and I also hear from bosses about the expectations for promotions that new employees have. They're asking in job interviews about when they can be promoted, and then they're pressuring in the first review for the next promotion. And my question is, "What's the rush?"

In some ways, I get it. When I was starting out, I was always looking ahead. I was anxious to snag my football scholarship and get to college. I rushed to get through grad school and be independent, out into the working world. But a lot of that had to do with a desire to liberate myself from the family home. Once in the workplace, I had no great expectations of rapid advancement until I had proven myself.

I think it's a little different today. When I entered the workplace, people didn't think entrepreneurially. They didn't look to start up a business, and they didn't manage their careers with a free-agent mindset. People went to work for a company, worked for a while, developed some skills, and went on from there.

Since that time, there have been many stories of people starting businesses, having their IPO and becoming billionaires. And maybe even changing the world, like Mark Zuckerberg did with Facebook. Not only is the model there but the whole enabling infrastructure of services is there as well, including the ability to start a business on a shoestring, whether online or otherwise.

So, a lot has changed – thinking has changed, success stories abound, and new technologies enable people to be entrepreneurs more easily. But again, I ask, "What's the rush?"

The fact is that you are likely to be working for a minimum of 40 years. Soon it will become increasingly common for people to live to 100, and retirement ages will similarly skew upward because of sustained vitality and financial need. Which means there's plenty of time to live out whatever your ambition might be for your career. Once again, take your time and enjoy the journey.

I can look back now and ask myself, "What was the rush?" (actually I know what my rush was...independence). But today, I don't lament that I didn't work harder or move quicker. If anything, I'd lament that I didn't take it slower and try out some crazy, different avenues earlier (in my case, maybe coaching, or starting my own business). When you're young, you (hopefully) have the luxury of trying things, while still being able to swerve back toward a traditional career track if needed. And believe me, people who are hiring tend to understand this sort of youthful experimentation; many wish they had had the courage to do it themselves.

So again, don't be in a rush to get through life...while our time on earth is relatively short in epochal terms, it's really a marathon. Think of it that way and enjoy the show. Remember, the pleasure is in the doing – in the process – so don't just think in terms of getting through it. Smell the roses, enjoy the journey, and take the long view.

"Don't try to rush things that need time to grow."
- Unknown

29

Never Miss a Chance to Celebrate

By now we know about stopping to smell the roses and embracing the journey...appreciating what we have. But now we're going to take that a step further.

I remember early in adulthood occasionally thinking to myself that I didn't really feel any great sense of accomplishment when I actually did achieve something notable. This despite the fact that I had gone through graduations, gotten awards, job promotions, and the like. Yet these things felt like they were no big deal. It was almost as if I was detached from them and what I had accomplished. I think my thought process was something like, "Of course you did that. You did the work and did it well." Typically, I was already focused on the next milestone.

I was so wrong. The only reason I didn't feel a sense of accomplishment is that, while growing up, my family didn't place an emphasis on celebrating achievements. Doing well was the expectation. What you *didn't* want was the attention associated with *not* doing well. So I didn't come from a culture of celebrating or enjoying life's successes.

My wife came from the opposite family culture. Her mother celebrated everything. When we got married, I suddenly found myself celebrating birthdays and achievements and milestones, or just about anything – pet birthdays, Groundhog Day, or maybe "just because". At first it seemed a little embarrassing, but then I came to appreciate it. Celebrations gave me a chance to stop and savor the moment, to reflect on accomplishments and to share that with my loving wife, who was only too happy to celebrate with me. So I've learned another lesson: Never miss a chance to celebrate anything.

There are several aspects of this I want to emphasize:

- You should take a moment and pat yourself on the back, or if possible, allow someone else to do it for you. You've earned it. Even if it's something like a birthday where all you've done to earn it is to keep breathing for another year, think of it as an opportunity to reflect. Be kind to yourself (see Shortcut #32) and let yourself enjoy the moment.
- If you allow someone else to lead the celebration (as I've learned to do with my wife), you're also letting them do something that makes *them* happy. And as we said, sharing a sunrise is more than twice as pleasurable as watching it alone.
- Circumstances can change in a moment, whether your health or the health of a loved one, your finances, or a pandemic. Yet we always assume things will get better, that we will progress in our career, that life will become more bountiful, and things will become easier. But what if it doesn't? What if this is as good as it gets? A little celebration is a good way to lock into memory an appreciation for the good things we do have in the moment.

- We're all worthy of a little celebration. Because there were few celebrations in my childhood, I somehow grew up with the feeling I wasn't worthy of that attention and it was unseemly to focus on myself. And I carried that along into adulthood. As cheesy as this may sound, I do believe we're all special in our own way. We're all worthy, and we're all deserving of taking a bow every once in a while.

I learned this not only from my wife but also from her mother, who doted on me. Because of them, I learned to actually enjoy little victories, whether my own or by celebrating those of others. We've incorporated this into our family culture and try to celebrate all of our daughter's successes. These feel fun and heartfelt, but they are also part of fostering her sense of self-worth.

I would even stretch this notion of celebrating to include things that haven't happened yet, like an upcoming vacation. In my single days I often took vacations on the spur of the moment, which often limited some of my options. My wife, on the other hand, plans vacations in advance, thinking them out to make sure we can enjoy the full range of possibilities. But the real benefit of this approach is the time it allows to savor the anticipation of the trip – it's like doubling the enjoyment of a vacation. So while you shouldn't miss a chance to celebrate after the fact, you can also celebrate in advance. Because why not?

"Celebrate what you want to see more of."
- *Tom Peters*

30

Stay Hungry, Stay Foolish

In the late '60's/early '70's there was a sort of counterculture magazine called the *Whole Earth Catalog* that featured articles and essays, and served as somewhat of a Bible for a restless generation. When it had run its course, its last issue featured a picture of a country road (symbolic of a journey) with the words, "Stay Hungry, Stay Foolish".

This strikes me as such an insightful bit of wisdom, on many different levels. It is a wonderful wish, and also a phrase that can provide guidance as we travel on our respective journeys.

Since you have no idea what I'm talking about, let's start with thinking about a life span. When you're born, you have nothing, you're naked, you're exposed, and you're completely dependent. But all you need is food, an occasional clean diaper, and some hugs. You make all kinds of unconscious and involuntary sounds as they occur to you. You have no cares in the world, you haven't been taught anything, and it's all good as long someone takes care of you. Fast forward to the end of your life and it's likely to be pretty much the same thing.

Everything in between is where life occurs, which is the subject of this book. But there are also lessons to be learned from the beginning and end points. As exhorted by the *Whole Earth Catalog*, hunger and foolishness is the natural state we humans are born into. We have nothing but hunger – for food, but also knowledge and understanding of this new world we've been thrust into. We also crave the people in our life who have been caring for us and providing all forms of nourishment. In this state, there is a sense of total wonder.

And since we haven't yet been taught anything and have no life experience, there's no sense of right or wrong, of what to do or not to do. There are no boundaries, which means we can do whatever occurs to us. There's nothing to lose and everything is on the table. As such, we can get away with anything. We are utterly foolish, and are completely expected to be such.

Can you imagine going through your whole life like that, hungry and foolish? Because a lot of those descriptions sound like attractive traits and ideals. A hunger for knowledge and new experiences? An openness that allows you to welcome new people into your life? A sense of wonder about new experiences and the world? No boundaries? Total spontaneity? Feeling like you have nothing to lose? Not being wary of the world after being hurt? No rules? Sign me up!

In reality, as we proceed on our journey, we gain knowledge and have experiences that connect us with the world and help us operate as a member of a society. But these also become limitations of sorts. There are many things we are taught not to do. There are expectations placed upon us by parents, peers, and society. We have experiences, some of which may be hurtful. We build up layers of armor to protect us from pain, but which can also restrict our movement and keep a lot of the world out, both good and bad.

Wouldn't it be great if we didn't need that armor or could shed it at will? If we could look at a new opportunity – or a new person – as if there were no expectations from others, no rules, no sense that we had anything to lose?

The fact is, life gets messy between the two endpoints. Life at times is hard. But the living is what we get to do with it all, both the challenges and the opportunities. We get to make our choices. We get to make it work for us. It is our one and only life.

Recalling some of the most blissful aspects of your earliest years can reopen up the possibilities. Remember, for instance, how you were grateful for every little thing, whether a cookie, a nap or a clean diaper? And then you got jaded by the world. Wouldn't it be wonderful if we remembered to be truly grateful for everything good that happens?

Remember what it was like when you just trusted the world and all the people in it? Experience teaches us to protect ourselves by reserving our trust until it is earned. This is for our own self-preservation. But, until proven otherwise, isn't trust a better place to operate from?

What about looking back to a time before you took yourself so seriously, when you were truly humbled by the vastness and the complexity of everything you saw around you? Staying humble is a good thing. Life is too serious to be taken seriously. Remember the lightness of youth, when nothing could be taken too seriously?

So imagine diving into something that strikes your fancy and pursuing it with all you've got, unconcerned for the reward or the consequences. Sounds like a great way to pursue a relationship, an interest, or a career. That's us in our natural state, unaffected by the world. That's your true self.

Hungry and foolish.

In fact Bob Dylan put it very succinctly in his song, "It's Alright, Ma (I'm Only Bleeding)", when he said, "He (who is) not busy being born is busy dying." Typically, we think of the physical act of being born happening only once, but Dylan refers to "being born" as a process that can and should occur continually throughout life. It's a metaphor for reinventing yourself, renewing yourself, shedding whatever is holding you back from the lightness of youth, looking at new horizons with wonder, and for reimagining. Because if you're not actively working on these forms of rebirth, if you're trying to stay in place with where you've been...then you're stagnating, and you're really just busy dying...waiting for the Grim Reaper. What's wonderful is that rebirth can occur at any point in life. If you've become self-satisfied or feel as if you've given up at 50, you can start dying spiritually and live a very challenging later life.

And what about later life, or, more accurately, end-of-life? Steve Jobs is very succinct and insightful on this part (Jobs faced a diagnosis of terminal pancreatic cancer, which ultimately did claim him). As he said in a 2005 Stanford commencement speech:

> ..."for the past 33 years, I have looked in the mirror every morning and asked myself: "If today were the last day of my life, would I want to do what I am about to do today?" And whenever the answer has been "No" for too many days in a row, I know I need to change something.

> Remembering that I'll be dead soon is the most important tool I've ever encountered to help me make the big choices in life. Because almost everything — all external expectations, all pride, all fear of embarrassment or failure — these things just fall away in the face of death, leaving only what is truly important. Remembering that you are going to die is the best way I know to avoid the trap of thinking

you have something to lose. You are already naked. There is no reason NOT to follow your heart.

He went on to say:

> Even people who want to go to heaven don't want to die to get there. And yet death is the destination we all share. No one has ever escaped it. And that is as it should be, because Death is very likely the single best invention of Life. It is Life's change agent. It clears out the old to make way for the new.
>
> Right now, the new is you, but someday not too long from now, you will gradually become the old and be cleared away. Sorry to be so dramatic, but it is quite true."

I can't say it better than that. Death is actually a perfect context to serve as a lens to view important matters in your life. Will my life be diminished if I don't have this person in my orbit? Is this a fact about me that I would want my friends or my kids to remember me by? What do I want it to say on my epitaph? Am I working toward doing what it is I want to be known for? And if not, what the heck am I doing?

Confucius said, "We have two lives, and the second begins when we realize we only have one." That is, we live a life full of naïve and idealistic illusions, thinking that our life is limitless. It is not until we get in touch with our mortality and our limitations – and see the world as it actually is – that we can do our true life's work. Our real life is when we become our best self, when we can do what's truly in our heart – something that will be most meaningful to us.

To put Confucius' "two lives" in a different context, we return to Bob Dylan, who, in the song "My Back Pages" said, "Ah, but I was so much older then, I'm younger than that now". He seemed to refer to an earlier time when he took himself too seriously, was looked upon as a prophet, and thought he had life figured out. Now he comes to realize how little of life's mystery he really understands, and as such, life (and the world) has opened up for him. I certainly relate to this – in my early adulthood I thought I had it all figured out, and most issues were pretty black-and-white to me. But now I've come to realize how close-minded I was, that most of life is grey, and what do I know, really? Who am I to judge? It's like being unchained, closer to the beginning of life ("busy being born"). Today, I truly do feel younger of mind and more open to the world than I did as a young adult, and it is a very liberating feeling.

The fact is, we're all going to die. We feel like we're destined for this blissful ocean voyage through life. We're all sailing away, enjoying this journey...but it turns out we're all on the Titanic. And we might think we're booked in First Class, or Third Class, or Steerage...but it really doesn't matter. All of us in this world, fundamentally we're really all the same, on the same journey, and all with the same fate.

Rather than that being a depressing thought, let it be a liberating one. The universe is not counting on you to be a savior. When your days are done, the good things *and* the bad things that you do will not (likely) make a dent in the course of mankind. You're only responsible for you...and the people in your life. Your life only has meaning to you and the people you touch. You can't live forever, and you only live beyond death through the people that remain. So do the things that make you happy, for your purposes, and for the people who mean the most to you.

Stay hungry, stay foolish.

> "'It's impossible,' said Pride. 'It's risky,' said Experience. 'It's pointless,' said Reason. 'Give it a try,' whispered the Heart."
>
> - Unknown

31

--- --- --- --- --- ---

The Power of Animals

I grew up in a household that was pretty much pet-free. We had a dog named Dusty for a few years when I was a toddler, but he was killed by a car. We had a couple of outdoor cats who came and went, and goldfish for a few years. But we were mainly without pets, and, as a child, I certainly never had the experience of truly bonding with a pet.

Interestingly enough, my three siblings and I all married animal lovers and all have had multiple-dog households. My wife and I have had two dogs and two cats at any given time for the majority of our marriage. And I love it. Apparently I was a latent animal lover and didn't know it.

When we were first married, my wife had two cats named Bow and Arrow – cats were practical for her mainly because they're easy to leave for a week of travel if needed. Arrow was generally a recluse around strangers but for some unknown reason, he took to me, followed me around and ultimately won me over. Cats tend to have interesting personalities – generally more interesting than dogs have – but Arrow had some really peculiar quirks that made him very endearing. With Arrow I was hooked, and when the dogs arrived, I was all in.

What I have learned is how much animals can add to your life. Some people immediately think of all the compromises...the fur all over the place, dealing with animal waste, the responsibility, the expense, the travel arrangements. Before I bonded with pets, I was in that camp. Now, I realize all of that is merely part of the deal, and some of these factors, like the responsibility, are actually good things. And the benefits far outweigh the minuses.

I look back very fondly on the days when I would walk our daughter to grade school with our two dogs in tow. They made many friends in the neighborhood. The school crossing guard was a dog lover and always had doggie treats in his pocket – we would always chat after I dropped off my daughter. That whole experience is a very happy memory for me to this day, with the dogs as key players.

When COVID hit, many people (wisely) adopted pets to add life, comfort and companionship to their households. We already had our two dogs, but they became a focal point as my daughter and I made a point of walking them together and spending that extra time together each day.

Given pets' distinctive personalities and their capers, they truly do become part of the family and its lore. Even our departed furry friends live on as we reminisce over some of their more notable escapades.

A full two-thirds of U.S. households, or 85 million families, have at least one pet. It's well known that, along with the immediate joys of companionship, pets bring many benefits for both physical and mental health. And this is not limited to dogs and cats – aquarium fish, birds and reptiles can also provide many similar benefits.

Playing with a dog or cat can elevate levels of serotonin and do-pamine, which help calm and relax us. Pet owners have lower tri-glyceride and cholesterol levels (indicators of heart disease) than those without pets. Heart attack patients with pets survive longer than those without. Pet owners over age 65 make 30 percent fewer visits to their doctors than those without pets. And there are any number of reasons why therapy dogs are commonly used in hospitals and care homes. [Per HelpGuide.org]

For one thing, pets fulfill the basic human need for touch. Even hardened criminals in prison show long-term changes in their behavior after interacting with pets, many of them experiencing mutual affection for the first time. Stroking, hugging, or other-wise touching a loving animal can rapidly calm and soothe you when you're stressed or anxious. The companionship of a pet can also ease loneliness, and most dogs are a great stimulus for healthy exercise, which can substantially boost your mood and ease depression.

Think about some of these health and wellness benefits: increas-ing exercise, providing companionship, helping you meet new people, reducing anxiety, adding structure and routine to your day, and providing sensory stress relief. Seems like the benefits far outweigh the inconvenience of having to scoop a little poop.

Pets can provide meaning and joy to otherwise isolated seniors. Children who grow up in a pet household learn responsibility, compassion and empathy. Studies have shown that receiving feed-back from a pet can boost a child's self-image. Kids who bond with their pets can more easily form relationships with other people. Pets can also calm a hyperactive or overly aggressive child.

And there are any number of other pet alternatives to the popular dogs and cats [again, per HelpGuide.org]:

- Snakes and lizards can actually grow attached to the people who care for them, inviting petting; they can be exotic and beautiful.
- Rabbits may be a good furry alternative for people who are allergic to dogs and cats, and with lower maintenance. They don't require much space, and petting them can reduce stress levels and increase serotonin, the "happy hormone."
- Birds may have very long lifespans (some parrots outlive humans), reducing the occasion of loss. They can be exotic, have a lot of personality, and you can even teach them tricks.
- You'll often find fish tanks in doctors' offices, care homes and other medical facilities. One reason: They've been shown to reduce stress and lower the heart rate.

If you've grown up around animals you probably already recognize the wonderful aspects of having pets in your life. For someone like myself who did not, it has been an amazing surprise.

Pets don't ask for much...just food and a little love. And in turn, they'll provide a lifetime of love, understanding and companionship, without asking questions.

> "Until one has loved an animal, a part of one's soul remains unawakened."
>
> *- Anatole France*

32

Be Kind to Yourself

While we often speak and think about the relationships in our lives, we don't often think about our relationship with ourself. "To love oneself," wrote Oscar Wilde, "is the beginning of a life-long romance." And I believe a healthy form of self-love should come before one tries to give love to another person.

We all have ups and downs in our lives, maybe all in a single day. It's easy for a sports fan to love their team when it's winning, but are they still there for the team when it hits a losing streak?

Similarly, self-esteem can come easily during good times, when our accomplishments are front and center. But when we have setbacks, self-esteem and self-love can be challenged. Suddenly we remember all our faults. Our self-talk can be dominated with tough judgements, including blaming and shaming. We may abandon ourselves, and look outside ourselves for whatever might offer comfort – other people, food, alcohol, shopping. As with the sports fan, the question becomes, Can you be there for "the home team" in the good times and the bad? Do you still love yourself after you've suffered a setback? Does your self-esteem continue to sustain you in the downtimes?

I know this territory well. A friend once observed, "You're your own judge, jury and executioner" ...and after thinking for a moment, I replied, "Yes, and prosecutor too...everything but the defense attorney". This is what happens when you want to be perfect, when you don't allow yourself to fail without recriminations. In fact, as we all know, nobody is perfect, and nobody should hold themselves to that standard, nor expect it. This is when we need a friend to love us, that friend being ourselves.

The Buddhists have a concept known as "self-compassion" that encapsulates how we can care for ourselves as we might do for a friend who is down. Buddha put it quite simply: "You can search the whole tenfold universe and not find a single being more worthy of love and compassion that the one seated here – yourself." Self-compassion and self-forgiveness are not weaknesses, but rather expressions of courage and strength. To put it simply, it involves what I like to refer to as, being kind to yourself...at all times, good times and bad. But especially during the bad.

Another popular expression is "love yourself" as you might love and nurture another person, or maybe a passion in your life. Isn't it ironic that we might know well how to love another person, but we either forget or don't know how to love ourselves? We're all worthy of being loved, so let's not forget to love ourself. In fact, our love for another person will be a lot healthier if we are whole unto ourselves – that is, if we first love and nurture ourselves.

How do we do this? Per lifestyle blogger and entrepreneur Marelisa Fabrega, here are some suggestions:

- Carve out some "me time" for yourself every day to do something that brings you joy. It could be writing, running, music, or anything you love to do.
- Give yourself recognition. Often, we're quick to acknowledge the achievements of others, but slow to acknowledge

our own. Become aware of your own achievements and give yourself a pat on the back. When you do something you're proud of, stop for a minute and dwell on it with a mental *Yay, me!*

- Cultivate your inner advocate. We're all familiar with the inner critic, that nasty little voice in our head that's quick to judge and always ready with a put down. But next time your inner critic comes at you with ridicule and scorn, welcome another voice: your inner advocate. This is the voice that jumps in and presents arguments on your behalf. Something like, "OK, nobody's perfect, glad to get that screwup out of the way and get back to doing it right". Or you might say, "Whoa, that was a doozy!", and have a laugh at your folly...and at how seriously you can take yourself.

- Forgive yourself. We all mess up, do things we're not proud of, fail to stand up for ourselves, or fail to follow through. Stop blaming yourself, resolve to do better going forward, and by all means, forgive yourself!

- Take good care of yourself; it's one of the best ways to show yourself kindness. Get enough sleep, eat healthy, and get some form of exercise on a regular basis. In addition, choose a way to release stress, and look after your appearance. These are all forms of loving yourself, and it's amazing what they will do for your state of mind.

- Respect yourself. Self-respect is valuing yourself for who you are, rather than allowing others to dictate your value. It's trusting yourself, thinking for yourself, forming your own opinions, and making your own decisions. In addition, it's refusing to compare yourself to others. Finally, self-respect is about keeping your promises to yourself and following through on what you tell yourself you're going to do.

- Treat yourself to something you've wanted, or do something that soothes you, like a hot bath or a quiet drive.

- Remind yourself of your good qualities and tell yourself, "I am enough." Maybe you're not good at everything (Who is?) or you're not exactly where you want to be. But you have a lot of great attributes, and you're plenty good just the way you are now.
- Stop trying to be perfect. Remember? The perfect is the enemy of the good. Nobody can be perfect, and, as a rule, good is good enough. Setting a standard of perfection is setting yourself up for failure. *Can you think of anything more unkind to do to yourself?*
- Believe in yourself. You've got all the personal resources you need to follow your dreams. You've got this.

Life is rewarding when we have loving people in our lives to sustain us and nurture our good attributes in good times and bad. But we're really at our best when we start from a place of doing that for ourselves with a healthy level of self-love and self-esteem. The relationship you build with yourself is one you will have for life. So, make it as healthy and loving as you can.

Don't be your own judge, jury and executioner. Be your own advocate. Be your own caregiver. Be your own consoler. Be your own cheerleader and coach. Be your own friend.

Be kind to yourself.

> "Remember you have been criticizing yourself for years and it hasn't worked. Try approving of yourself and see what happens."
>
> *- Louise L. Hay*

33

Be Nice

If "Think" is the motto of this book, I want to offer "Be Nice" as the mantra. No, we're not going to meditate today, but it can be used as a repetitive chant to remind you, or as a rallying cry for a great way to approach the world. Being nice is great for the world and great for you.

Let's look at a few trends in our society to put this into perspective:

- The more we rely on analytics and machine-based algo-rithms (i.e., AI) for decision-making, the more the human element is removed from decision-making. That means we are relying on the algorithm-makers to take all human or societal-related factors into account – and as a result, the unquantifiable and subjective human factors can't help but suffer as to being part of the analysis.
- The more we rely on social media and devices for com-munication, the less actual human interaction takes place. And the more we get used to impersonal interactions, the easier it is to avoid human contact.
- The less actual human contact we have, the less we un-derstand each other.

- The more impersonal and removed we become, the easier it is to take actions that might offend others or not fully take societal impact into account.
- There are too many forces trying to divide us for their own interests – not only political interests but also commercial interests, including services that target market to various interest groups, sensational reporting, etc. Is their priority in serving our interests, or their own?

Keeping all this in mind, all of us need to actively work at maintaining a sufficient level of humanity in our world. It's more important today to think in terms of humanity than at any other time in history.

"Be Nice" is my wish for you, and also a suggestion for a way to be. Because, being nice isn't only a positive way to interact with the world, it's also a healthy way for you to be with yourself. Being nice and thinking well of people around you has a calming and positive effect on your own well-being, too.

Think of the alternative. When you are angry, everyone around you will feel that anger, and it will have a negative impact (yes, we all have the power to impact people around us, and sometimes that power is much more than we imagine, both for better and for worse). At a minimum, your anger will knock them a bit off their game and arouse negative energy. Anger can also have a negative effect on yourself, robbing you of energy and filling your mind with gloomy, non-constructive thoughts.

Of course, anger is a natural emotion or state that we all experience, and sometimes rightly so – along with negative emotions such as irritability, frustration, loss, failure, jealousy. It's not necessary (or healthy) to eliminate or even to deny these feelings, but rather to be aware of how they affect our outlook while also impacting others. We can limit the impact. We can say our mantra, "Be Nice," and move on to a better place.

It's easy to get caught up in your own head when you're angry or frustrated. "Be Nice" will remind you of the world around you and the many opportunities to make a positive impact every day.

A few relevant quotes (by this point, you know I love smart quotes!) from a wide range of personalities who emphasize the point:

- "Too often we underestimate the power of a touch, a smile, a kind word, a listening ear, an honest compliment, or *the smallest act of caring*, all of which have the potential to turn a life around."

  Leo Buscaglia

- "The smallest act of kindness is worth more than the greatest intention."

  Kahlil Gibran

- "Happiness is the new rich.
  Inner peace is the new success.
  Health is the new wealth.
  Kindness is the new cool."

  Syed Balkhi

- "I've been searching for ways to heal myself, and I've found that kindness is the best way."

  Lady Gaga

- "Kindness is a language which the deaf can hear and the blind can see."

  Mark Twain

We all have an idea of how to "Be Nice." It involves staying calm, being positive and thinking positively of others around us – and tuning in to how others might be feeling. It's about considering how you might help someone in need. Being constructive. It's about asking how it's going and what you can do to help. So reach out to someone who matters to you, preferably someone you haven't spoken to in ages. Get involved in a positive cause that's meaningful to you. Smile at a stranger on the street. There are countless ways to be nice.

And while we can't do all of these acts of kindness all the time, we can do them more often. Repeating our mantra will remind us, so we can make being nice a regular thing. At a time when our society can use a little more humanity, you (and I) can be the change.

That's my wish for you. Be nice to each other. Be kind to yourself. Be nice.

> "When you are kind to others, it not only changes you, it changes the world."
>
> *- Rabbi Harold Kushner*

Acknowledgments

I am thankful to my parents, JoAnne and Frank, for teaching me right from wrong, instilling in me a love of learning, for protecting me and supporting me. And I thank my siblings, Gayle, Jim and Joe, and my broader family for all the love and support. And let's not forget my "family" of friends who provide a sense of warmth, comfort, renewal and context to my life.

Given all that, I think I've learned most of what I actually know about life from my experiences with my wife and with my daughter. They have been an ongoing source of inspiration, comfort, support, joy, honesty and stimulation, as well as the inspiration for this book idea. As I said, both of these women have helped determine the kind of person I've turned out to be, for the better.

I knew nothing about turning out a book when I started this project during the height of the global pandemic, and it took a team to get this one to see the light of day. Thanks to my students at Seton Hall University's Stillman School of Business for their enthusiastic response to my lessons, which gave me encouragement. Thanks to my friend and author Bill Goss who helped plant the idea for "a" book and shared his own experiences. Thanks to my friend and former classmate, Andy Robin, who generously shared his journey in self-publishing and the resources he used along the way (you can check out his book on retirement strategies, *Tapas Life*).

Immeasurable thanks go to my editor, Paula Derrow, who turned my words into what I really hoped for them to sound like. More importantly, she tapped into what made this project a meaningful thing for me to do, and translated that into what might make it meaningful for other people to read. Along with her editing ability, her encouragement and good judgment were indispensable and very much appreciated.

Similarly, I can't thank my designer, Cynthia Searight, enough for turning my thoughts and personality into the most appropriate visual packaging of the book and web presence. She always knew what I wanted before I knew. To work with her is to have all the resources of a great marketing agency at hand...one that always says, "yes, we can." Her enthusiasm for the project and energy played a vital role in helping to get the project across the finish line in strong fashion.

This book (and my life) has been enhanced by a lot of awesome people. I am a very fortunate person.

About the Author

David Graziano was born in Maryland before Kennedy and the Cuban Missile Crisis, and grew up in Ohio and New Jersey. He lamely flirted with his future wife-to-be in seventh-grade homeroom, but his primary focus was on playing any game that had a ball. He also hustled odd jobs in the neighborhood, and still has those first dollars, stashed in a drawer or wherever...

He earned a full football scholarship to attend Villanova University where he was a Summa Cum Laude engineering student, team captain and two-time Academic All-American. He then attended Harvard Business School, where he earned his MBA.

He describes his postgraduate years as his "so-called career" or, more aptly, his "collection of experiences." It is roughly broken down as 20 years of corporate work in computer-related businesses, and 20 years of other stuff, including business consulting, dad, coach and college professor. In the middle of all that, at 42, he married his seventh-grade sweetheart (it only took him 30 years to figure out what she knew at 12). They were very blessed to have a daughter a few years later. And this is when the real living began.

Learn more at www.towardhappyandfulfilled.com.

Made in United States
Orlando, FL
22 January 2022

13894607R00098